P9-CBI-908

Unplug the Christmas Machine

☆ Unplug the Christmas Machine

How to Have the Christmas You've Always Wanted

Jo ROBINSON & Jean Coppock STAEHELI

William Morrow and Company, Inc. + New York + 1982

Library of Congress Cataloging in Publication Data

Robinson, Jo.
Unplug the Christmas machine.

Bibliography: p.
1. Christmas. 2. Simplicity. 3. Christmas decorations. 4. Christmas—United States.
I. Staeheli, Jean Coppock. II. Title.
GT4985.R62 1982 394.2′68282 82-12465
ISBN 0-688-01319-8
ISBN 0-688-01461-5 (pbk)

Printed in the United States of America

2 3 4 5 6 7 8 9 10

BOOK DESIGN BY MARIA EPES

We dedicate this book to
all the people who have shared their
Christmas stories with us.

Authors' Note

This book is based largely on the insights, problems, and solutions of people who have graciously shared an important part of their lives with us. We are in the process of gathering information on how people feel about *all* the recognized holidays—Christian and non-Christian—as well as birthdays and other family events. If you have a special way of observing a holiday or a holiday-related problem or just want to air your views, please write to us at Family Celebrations, P.O. Box 06517, Portland, OR 97206.

Acknowledgments

First and foremost, we are grateful to our husbands, Bruce and Michael, for their good-natured financial and emotional support and for their unflagging belief in our never-ending projects. Our special thanks go to Pat McGrady for guiding us through the labyrinth of the publishing world and to Mike McGrady, our mentor, who made this book possible. We are indebted to our editor, Maria Guarnaschelli, for giving us the courage of our convictions and for her vital enthusiasm. Our thanks to Anne Smith, editor in chief of *Redbook* magazine, for her personal interest in our project and for her sensitivity to the needs of women. The Reverend Newton Roberts, friend and Christian education consultant for the Presbytery of the Cascades, has earned our gratitude for his assistance in making the *Leader's Guide* to our "Unplug the Christmas Machine" workshop available to churches around the country. Thanks to the Reverend Randy Riggs, associate pastor of Westminster Church in Portland, Oregon, for his interest in restoring the meaning of Christmas. We are grateful to Bill Moyers for his belief in our work. Rena Grossfield deserves special mention for her clipping service, her publishing know-how, and her guided tours through the streets of New York City. Bob and Joan Burns have shown us gracious hospitality during our trips to New York. And thank you, Karen Norris, for joining forces with Robinson/Staeheli Enterprises when all we had to offer were our ideas and enthusiasm.

Table of Contents

Introduction: Christmas Lost and Found

Christmas. The very word means joy. When people have a wonderful day or a delightful surprise, they are apt to say: "This feels just like Christmas!" Unfortunately, the holiday itself is not living up to its promise. Within this century, Christmas has changed from a delightful folk festival and an important religious celebration to a twenty-billion-dollar-a-year commercial venture. Each December, millions of Americans find themselves spending more money than they can really afford, taking on more responsibilities than they can comfortably handle, and spending less relaxed time with their families than at any other time of the year. Some people have more problems with Christmas than just a mild feeling of tiredness and a thick stack of bills. Every holiday season there's a 15 percent increase in the number of people seeking professional help for depression. And debt counselors report that the bulk of their clients come to them in February, when the holiday bills arrive.

Christmas has become a national neurosis. Yet no one has given the celebration the in-depth investigation it deserves. Each news medium has its own limited response to the holiday. Business magazines issue their annual forecasts of Christmas profits. Newspapers feature weeks of practical advice for the homemaker. Traditional women's magazines compete with each other in turning out their most bountiful Christmas issues ever. And talk shows extend yearly invitations to local psychologists to give their prescription for "the Christmas Blues."

The larger story remains untold. What is it really like to go through the holiday season in an American family today? What lies at the bottom of most people's problems with Christmas? And more important, what can people do to restore the simplicity and beauty of the celebration?

Since 1978 we've been talking to thousands of people to find answers to these questions. We began our exploration of Christmas when we were asked by an Oregon college to design a one-day workshop to help families plan a less stressful, more rewarding Christmas. We based our workshop on a simple self-discovery process that enables the participants to pinpoint their problems, define their values, explore their wishes and dreams, and combine all these insights into a workable plan. Over the next four years we gave this workshop for a variety of groups, including churches of seven major denominations, child development specialists, members of the clergy, Christian educators, community colleges, parents' groups, professional women's groups, and businesses. No matter whom we talked to, we were always impressed by how much people care about Christmas. When they talked openly about the celebration, they explored their spiritual lives, their hopes and dreams for their children, the state of their marriages, their relationships with relatives, and their family finances. Christmas brings together the most important elements of people's lives.

Because of this rare opportunity to listen to so many people exploring their family celebrations, we've been able to get some insight into what is wrong with the American way of Christmas. Clearly, Christmas is becoming ever more commercial, expensive, hectic, pressured, impersonal, and materialistic. And we've had a chance to see to what degree the financial exploitation of the holiday has altered the very nature of the celebration, robbing it of vitality and meaning.

As we will show throughout this book, Christmas is dramatically different now from what it was a hundred years ago. First, the natural rhythm of the holiday has been altered. In the nineteenth century, families rarely began holiday preparations before mid-December, but the celebration itself lasted for days. Today, people are encouraged to shop for the holiday months in advance, but once the holiday selling is over, the festivities end abruptly. Christmas has become a long and elaborate preparation for an intense gift-opening ritual.

Second, folk and religious traditions nurtured for centuries have been replaced with passive, moneymaking events. For example, the family game-playing, dancing, and music-making that were as important to our ancestors as the presents have been supplanted by spectator sports and trips to decorated shopping malls.

Third, the family Christmas celebration has become an elaborate and expensive production. Originally on a par with Thanksgiving, it now takes far more of a family's time, energy, and money than any other annual event. Every year people are encouraged to think that they have to spend more and do more to get the same amount of satisfaction.

Our workshop transcripts and interviews offer sad testimony to how often the commercialized spectacle of the Christmas Machine and the best interests of the family are in conflict. Busy women are encouraged to stage a grand-production Christmas requiring weeks of added effort, and are given the subtle message that their families' happiness depends on their performance. Men find themselves without a meaningful part to play in a celebration that to them seems too elaborate and out of their control. And children are the prime targets of the Christmas Machine, which turns their joyous anticipation of the holiday into an obsession with name-brand toys.

But not all of the problems people have with Christmas can be blamed on holiday commercialism. The facts of family life have been changing and this requires a reevaluation of the basic assumptions people have about Christmas. More and more people are living alone, more women than ever are working outside the home, families are smaller, there are more single parents, and male and female roles have been largely redefined. A celebration based on large family gatherings, traditional family configurations, and stereotyped sex roles may no longer correspond to people's changing needs, values, and circumstances.

For these two reasons—because commercialism has eaten away at the vitality of the celebration and because families are going through such radical changes—people can no longer rely on habit or the passive acceptance of a prepackaged Christmas for a rewarding celebration. They must define for themselves what they value about Christmas and create a celebration that meets their families' unique needs.

ABOUT THIS BOOK

We have written this book to help people create more rewarding Christmas celebrations. In the first four chapters, we take a closer look at how Christmas affects family life. We show how women's changing lives are often at odds with their traditional role at Christmas. We look at the limited participation of men in the holiday and how this lessens their enjoyment. We explore the four things children really want—and don't always get—for Christmas. And we show how the changing makeup of the family has affected the traditional Christmas reunion. Then, in the rest of the book, we examine the central components of the American way of Christmas—the elaborate gift-giving, the trend toward a spectacular celebration, and the passive consumption of "holiday events"—and show why they often don't work for families today.

But in addition to discussing the problems people have with Christmas, we help readers find their own solutions through a series of exercises based on our original workshop, and by exploring a wide range of possible alternatives. One of our most definite conclusions is that there is no one "right" way to celebrate Christmas. People find meaning and enjoyment in the holiday in highly individual ways. But within this rich diversity, we've discovered one common denominator: the people who find the most pleasure in Christmas are the ones who have taken control of the celebration and shaped it to conform to their own wishes and values. They know what's most important about Christmas to them and they've found ways to make those values come alive.

It is easier than most people think to add life and meaning to their celebrations. We have helped thousands of people turn a disappointing holiday into a festival of renewal. You carry within you the seeds of a good Christmas, and no matter how commercial Christmas has become or how trapped you may feel in an unsatisfying routine, you can regain control of your own celebration. In just a few hours of reflection, you will see what you need to do to create the Christmas you really want. Even if you pick up this book the week before Christmas, you will still be able to find ways to make the holiday more enjoyable.

At the back of each chapter there is a question and answer section, where we give advice on dealing with specific problems, such as:

- ☆ How can I recapture the joy of an old-fashioned Christmas?
- ☆ How can I share my holiday values with my children?
- ☆ How can I have a rich celebration without straining the family budget?
- ☆ How can I nurture the spiritual side of my celebration?
- ☆ How can I keep my recent divorce from spoiling the family Christmas?
- ☆ What can I do at Christmas to help people who are less fortunate?
- ☆ How can I entertain my family and friends without making it a huge production?

☆ How can I save time on holiday preparations and still give my family a memorable Christmas?
☆ How can I get my husband more involved in Christmas?
☆ How can we have more fun at our Christmas reunion?

To answer these questions, we've drawn on the most innovative ideas of the present and the most lasting ideas of the past. And we've gathered information from people all around the country who have found unique ways to celebrate. The book concludes with an appendix that contains hundreds of additional specific suggestions for having a wonderful holiday without spending enormous amounts of time, money, and effort. (Where prices of particular items are given for guidance, we have tried to make them as up-to-date as possible, but of course they are subject to change at any time.)

After reading this book, you will probably discover that you want to hold on to most of your current practices and traditions. Very few of the people who have gone through our workshop have felt a need to abandon their traditions entirely and start all over again. In fact, this book will most likely give you renewed appreciation for many of the things you are already doing, while inspiring you to make a few simple changes that will make all the difference in your enjoyment of Christmas.

Merry Christmas!

The Christmas Pledge

Believing in the beauty and simplicity of Christmas, I commit myself to the following:

1. *To remember those people who truly need my gifts*

2. *To express my love for family and friends in more direct ways than presents*

3. *To rededicate myself to the spiritual growth of my family*

4. *To examine my holiday activities in light of the true spirit of Christmas*

5. *To initiate one act of peacemaking within my circle of family and friends*

☆

CHAPTER 1:

Women: The Christmas Magicians

When we listen to people talking about Christmas, often the first thing they mention is holiday commercialism. Almost everyone is distressed by what they see happening to the celebration. But very quickly, the conversation turns to how Christmas affects their families. What really matters to people is the quality of their own celebrations. So in the first few chapters of this book we'll be taking a look at the Christmas pageant from the viewpoint of each member of the family.

There's no better place to start than with women, because the whole celebration seems to revolve around them. Like their mothers before them, they are the Christmas Magicians, responsible for transforming their family's everyday lives into a beautiful, magical festival. A fifty-year-old woman named Marilyn shared with us her memories of her mother's vital part in her childhood Christmases. "When my mother opened the door on Christmas," she said, "I knew exactly what was going to happen. I knew that she would decorate the house on December 17, the day after my brother's birthday. I knew that we would have oyster stew for Christmas Eve dinner. And I knew that she would go to great trouble to get both me and my brother the one gift we really pined for." And in her own family, Marilyn found herself playing the same key role. "My husband tells me that I *am* Christmas," she said.

Because of this central role, women have the satisfaction of giving their families a wonderful Christmas, and for many women, this celebration is the consummate expression of their skill, not only in the craft of homemaking, but also in the art of loving. But being Christmas Magicians also gives them most of the work and the worry. In most families, women are the holiday planners, organizers, hostesses, decorators, shoppers, housecleaners, and bakers. With so much to do, it's no wonder that many of them go through the holiday season with conflicting feelings of joy and pressure. These mixed feelings come out at the very beginning of our workshops, when we ask people to write down the first three words that come to mind when they think about the holiday. In one workshop, ten women volunteered these typical, mixed responses: "rushed, overwhelmed, joy"; "Christmas tree, happy, stressful"; "rushed, children, disappointment"; "fear, anticipation, excitement"; "church, fun, hectic"; "procrastination, joy, values"; "family, Jesus, tired"; "travel, excited, worried"; "gifts, tree, stressful"; "love, family, expectant."

One of the women in this group was surprised to find that she had written down completely opposite words. "I wrote down 'stressful' and 'happy'!" said Karen, a twenty-five-year-old artist and the mother of two young children. "And I love Christmas. Or I thought I did." Karen explained that she was excited about Christmas because it gave her a chance to make gifts for her family and get together with all of her brothers and sisters. But when she thought about why she had written down "stressful," she realized she rarely had the time to do all the things she wanted in a relaxed fashion. "I'm just starting to wrap a package when my husband walks in the door and I don't even know what I'm cooking for dinner," she said.

Karen got a better understanding of why she was always pressed for time at Christmas when we asked her to examine a list of holiday chores and check the ones that she was primarily responsible for—things like making up a gift list, shopping, sending cards, helping at church, baking, decorating, preparing for houseguests, and so forth. Karen found herself checking more than twenty items and suddenly gained a new appreciation of all the things she was trying to accomplish. (The complete list appears in the exercises at the end of this chapter.)

Like Karen, many women underestimate all the extra effort that's involved in their family celebrations. While they know full well that they are busier than usual in December, and are aware of obvious tasks like buying gifts, most of them overlook dozens of less visible chores. For example, few women stop to consider all the separate steps involved in gift-giving. They often spend weeks thinking up creative gift ideas, shopping for bargains, going out of their way to specialty stores, doing original wrapping, and taking care of the mailing details. When all of their separate holiday tasks are added together, many women find that getting ready for Christmas feels like a part-time job.

One of the reasons few women realize how much extra work they do every Christmas is that they don't view most of their special chores as "work." They find an element of pleasure in almost all of them. In fact, many women look forward all year long to the holiday sewing, baking, and decorating. But what they rarely take into account is that they often have to do these things under less than ideal conditions. When they look back to the previous year, they see that they were buying gifts on lunch hour, trying to bake cookies with their children at the same time as they were cooking dinner and cleaning the house, wrapping gifts late into the night, and writing cheery notes on Christmas cards even while paying overdue bills. It's easy to see how even the most enjoyable holiday activities can become burdensome when packed into such a tight schedule.

When women see all that they're trying to do at Christmas, many of them wish for an extra two weeks. *Then* they could carry out all of their special traditions and projects and have the peace of mind to enjoy them. But few women have this luxury. They're working mothers, or single parents. They have demanding careers, or a houseful of children. One way or another their lives are full to begin with. And they often have to find time for Christmas by doing two things at once, staying up late, or eliminating those few unscheduled hours they count on to restore their energy.

Another aspect of their holiday role that many women fail to take into account is all the extra love and concern they pour into their families throughout the Christmas season. Women are so much more than assembly-line workers cranking out mince pies, wrapped gifts, and ornaments. They also put great effort into the dozens of invisible details that make the entire season a wonderful time for the family. They plan events that will surprise and delight everyone, try to anticipate problems in the family reunion before they arise, negotiate behind the scenes with strong-willed relatives, and attempt to take into consideration each person's needs and preferences during the holiday season. And throughout it all, they buoy up all the people around them with their spirit and enthusiasm. As rewarding as all of this may be, it does require considerable thought and energy.

During the height of the holiday season, we talked with a forty-five-year-old woman named Susan who gave us an indication of all the considerations that can go through a woman's mind as she prepares for her family Christmas reunion. She told us that for several days she had been cleaning the house, making the beds, shopping for groceries, and laying in a store of baked goods. And all the while, she had been mentally working on solutions to the following problems: How could she tactfully persuade her husband to pay more attention to his mother-in-law? How could she entertain her fourteen-year-old niece, who was going to be the only teen-ager at the family reunion? How could she make life easier for her youngest sister, who had a two-year-old and a brand-new baby? How could she shield her eighty-five-year-old grandfather from the noise and chaos of so many young children? And how could she arrange the eating schedule so that her diabetic father would have small and frequent meals?

Many of the women we've talked to devote exactly this kind of emotional energy to the family Christmas. And overall, it gives them a great deal of satisfaction to put so much thought into making Christmas a wonderful time for their families. But few women give themselves full credit for all the planning, caring, and thinking involved. When women have a better sense of both the physical and the emotional demands of their holiday role, they see more clearly how their joy in the celebration can be diluted by stressful feelings: they are adding weeks of effort and devotion to an already full schedule.

For many women, these extra holiday responsibilities impose only occasional moments of stress and overtiredness. By and large, they enjoy their holiday activities, and all they may need to do to find even more enjoyment in the celebration is to look for ways to scale down their responsibilities, to become better organized, or to seek more help.

Some women, however, find that being the Christmas Magicians gives them inexplicable feelings of anxiety as well. For example, a woman named Chris came to our workshop because she was always disappointed in herself at Christmas. "There's this image in my head," she said. "Five little stockings hanging on the mantel. A tree decorated with gingerbread cookies and hand-sewn ornaments. But everything around me is screaming out: 'You're not measuring up! You're not measuring up!' Even my cookies don't turn out like they're supposed to."

Chris felt as if the holiday put her on stage, making all of her domestic talents—or lack of them—highly visible. The rest of the year, what she did for her family seemed less important. But at Christmas, when her private home became an open house, the holiday seemed to test her graciousness as a hostess, her thoroughness as a housecleaner, her artistry as a craftsman, her sensitivity as a gift-giver, and her talent as a decorator. Although many women thrive on this challenge, Chris went through the season seeing everything she did through the eyes of a critical observer.

Christmas craft magazines can unwittingly add to the self-consciousness women like Chris feel at Christmas. Open up a typical December issue and there's a sumptuous vision of the beautiful Christmas a woman could give her family if only she worked long and hard enough. The magazines are filled with "helpful" advice on how she can transform her home into a winter wonderland, outdo herself as a craftsman, delight everyone on her gift list, dazzle her boss at the office party, and entertain with elegance and grace.

For example, a 1981 women's magazine devoted two full pages to encouraging women to fill every nook and cranny of their homes with Christmas ornaments made out of muslin. All told, the elaborate cloth creations required the combined talents of six professional artists and designers. Readers were invited to make muslin dolls, muslin Christmas stockings decorated with ribbon trellises, white-on-white ruffled coverlets and pillows, muslin baskets, and fabric trees and candles. "But don't stop there!" urged the editors. How about "lace-inset teardrop trims and soft floral triangles that repeat our stocking motifs," crowning a mantel with spectacular muslin fans and transforming muslin into a Madonna and Child?

For women who can pick and choose wisely from all of the possibilities the magazines offer, they can be a valuable resource and a welcome incentive. Holiday craft and baking projects have their definite place in the celebration—they add beauty, originality, and excitement to the holiday. But they are not essential to a good family Christmas. In fact, they can draw energy away from more important matters. What many women need to hear from the magazines is that they can give their families an equally good or even better Christmas by doing less. A friend of ours said it best: "I want to be excited by Christmas, and do a hundred projects if I feel like it. But I know that if I keep it simple, I'm not cheating myself or my family."

Ann, a working mother in her thirties, found out what her family really wanted from her at Christmas the hard way. She told us that she used to feel like a "bad mother" unless she made something from the magazines every Christmas. But two years ago she had reason to change her mind. That year she decided to make a marshallow castle that was on the cover of a craft magazine. The directions for the castle assured her that it was a "traditional project that would add so much to a festive season" and would provide the "focal point of your holiday decorating" as well. But things didn't turn out that way.

First of all, even though the directions said that the ingredients were inexpensive, she spent over seventeen dollars at the grocery store, which was much more than she could really afford. Second, the editors claimed that the project was simple enough for a child to complete, but Ann spent ten frustrating hours putting it together. The hardest part for her was making the turrets surrounding the castle. The directions told her to paste peppermint candies to four vertical cardboard tubes with marshallow crème. While the peppermints clung valiantly to the cardboard for a few hours, they oozed off during the night. When she woke up in the morning, she was greeted by a sagging castle surrounded by four half-naked toilet-paper tubes.

But the thing that really disappointed Ann was her family's reaction. She said that her husband took one look at it and told her that it was the ugliest thing he had ever seen. "He didn't even want it in the house," she said. And although the magazine told her that the "children would have hours of fun playing with the marshmallow knights and damsels that inhabit the magic castle," all *her* children wanted to do was eat them.

That experience taught her that she needed to look more carefully at her talents and interests and to be more selective about how she spent her time. "This year I'm going to spend that time with my children, instead," she said. "That's what they really want from me, anyway."

All of our interview material supports Anne's conclusion. In talking with men and children, we've found it to be invariably

true that what they really want for Christmas is a house filled with love and acceptance, not a house decorated to perfection. And friends and relatives often find it refreshing to be around someone who has voluntarily taken herself out of the beautiful-house competition.

When women have an accurate picture of all that they do at Christmas and then think about what's really important to them and their families, many of them come to the conclusion that they want Christmas to be simpler. Shirley, a teacher at a Presbyterian church and the mother of four children, put it most succinctly: "I found out that I couldn't care so much about the way Christmas looked and have it feel any good."

Shirley told us that years ago, she used to grab every moment of spare time to sew, bake, decorate, and write Christmas cards. "I was too busy to even question why I was doing it." But then something happened to make her examine her values. Shirley explained that her eighty-year-old mother had been living with her and was upset with herself because she didn't feel useful anymore. Her eyes were failing and she couldn't knit the kids sweaters for Christmas. She had very little money so she couldn't buy presents for the family. "I kept telling her that she didn't have to do or buy anything," Shirley said, "that Christmas was a time to enjoy being with the family. But she wouldn't listen to me."

During that holiday season, Shirley had a revelation. "I sat down one night, absolutely exhausted from all I was doing, and took a long look at myself. There I was, trying to do all the things my mother used to do at Christmas and more. I was also busy at church. I had hardly a moment to be with my family. My own advice to my mother hit me like a sledgehammer. I suddenly realized that all that is required of us is to exist with God."

At that point, Christmas started to become a relaxed affair at Shirley's house. Instead of writing Christmas cards, she wrote one letter each Sunday of Advent to a person who had special meaning for her. She stopped trying to make the tree a thing of beauty for other people and let the children help decorate it. "Everyone laughs at me because I'm always running to a drawer on Christmas morning to get a present that I neglected to wrap. But they all have a much better time than they used to when I was a nervous wreck."

Shirley ended her story with this simple comment: "It's not that I'm lazy. If I believed it would make my family truly happy, I'd work nonstop on Christmas. It's just that I've finally realized what's important."

Shirley had strong spiritual beliefs that steered her in the direction of a simple Christmas. Most women who find ways to take the stress out of Christmas make a less dramatic change. They make one or two simple adjustments and discover that this helps them feel more in control of the celebration and gives them more energy for their traditional activities. For example, one woman who attended our workshop found that all she had to do to feel more relaxed at Christmas was to cut down on her baking. "It was the fourth pie crust that used to get to me," she said. "Now I just make one or two pies for Christmas dinner and the whole family finds that this is more than enough."

By talking with hundreds of women, we've found that there is no one holiday role that works for all women. Some enjoy the challenge of a grand celebration. Some find that a simple Christmas works best for them. And others like the freedom to vary what they do from year to year depending on their circumstances. But to make the right choice, women need a wide range of options and the freedom to define for themselves what their role is to be. In the exercises that follow, you will have a chance to examine your present holiday role and explore some possible changes. Then there are answers to specific questions women have about Christmas.

Exercises for Women

Exercise 1: LIFE-STYLE INVENTORY

Many women overestimate the time they have available for holiday projects. Take the following life-style inventory to get a sense of how busy you are before you add on the responsibilities of Christmas.

1. Check all the following statements that are true for you:

I'm employed full-time.

I'm employed part-time.

I have young children who are not yet in school or daycare.

I have children in school or daycare.

I'm a student.

I'm a single parent.

I have extended-family obligations.

I am primarily responsible for managing the household.

I have the following additional commitments:

Church

School

Volunteer work (boards, charities, committees, etc.)

Children's activities

Classes

Other

2. As a general rule I can count on ____ hours of free time a day.

3. I usually spend those unscheduled hours in the following ways:

4. To find time to prepare for Christmas I usually take time from:

By taking this inventory, a woman named Cindy discovered that she had approximately two hours of free time a day, between nine and eleven at night. Cindy was a secretary and the mother of three children, so she often spent this time watching television or relaxing with her husband to recuperate from the routine demands on her. In order to fit in her holiday responsibilities, she had to give up this free time, try to do more than one thing at once, or stay up later than usual.

Exercise 2: EXAMINING THE WORK OF CHRISTMAS
This exercise will help you gain a more objective view of all the holiday responsibilities you may be adding to your everyday schedule.

1. Look at the following list of typical holiday responsibilities and place a check by the ones that you were primarily responsible for last year.

☆ Making up a gift list
☆ Christmas shopping
☆ Making gifts
☆ Wrapping gifts
☆ Mailing gifts
☆ Writing cards
☆ Making cards
☆ Helping out at church
☆ Holiday baking
☆ Home decorations
☆ Sewing clothes
☆ Special holiday cleaning
☆ Buying stocking stuffers
☆ Advent preparations
☆ Getting the tree
☆ Decorating the tree
☆ Outside decorations
☆ Hosting parties
☆ Preparing company meals
☆ Helping with school activities
☆ Planning family gatherings
☆ Making Christmas dinner
☆ Extra grocery shopping
☆ Making travel arrangements
☆ Packing
☆ Preparing for houseguests
☆ Other

2. Add any tasks that we have overlooked.

3. Spend some time remembering how you felt last Christmas as you were doing each of the chores that you checked. Put a star by the ones that you actually enjoyed.

4. Take a piece of paper and write down the tasks from the above list that you did not enjoy doing last year. Beside each one, write down a few words that describe the reason(s) for your dissatisfaction. Here are some common reasons:

Not enough time
Not enough money
Not enough family support
Not enough help
Don't enjoy this kind of activity
Don't value this kind of activity
My performance didn't measure up to my expectations
Wasn't creative enough

Cindy, the working mother we talked about in regard to the Life-style Inventory, made the following table:

Activity I didn't enjoy	*Reasons*
Making up gift list	Wasn't creative enough; wanted more help
Mailing gifts	Don't enjoy it; not enough time
Decorating tree	Had disagreement with husband; tree didn't look as good as I had hoped
Cooking holiday food	Not enough time; wanted more help
Buying gifts	Not enough time or money; too many gifts; did it myself

From this exercise, Cindy learned that there were several reasons she didn't enjoy some of her traditional holiday responsibilities, but the one that came through loud and clear was that she wanted more help. Another woman took this exercise and came to a different conclusion. Her main difficulty was that she was overly critical of everything she did, so she resolved to take on fewer projects and try to be more accepting of herself.

By completing these two exercises, you now have gained a better idea of how much time you have available for holiday projects, how much you attempt to do each Christmas, and how you feel about those tasks. Later chapters will give you an opportunity to examine your values and think about how simple or elaborate you want Christmas to be. These additional considerations will help you decide whether or not you want to make any changes in your holiday role.

Questions and Aswers

Question 1: *My family doesn't seem to notice all that I do for Christmas. Why can't they be more appreciative?*

Answer: In a workshop we gave for a professional women's group in 1980, one woman told us that she thought that many of her holiday problems would vanish if she got more words of appreciation: "My fantasy is that I awake in my husband's arms, and he is kissing me and telling me how wonderful I am. How many of us hear that? 'Gee, you're wonderful. What a wonderful Christmas dinner. Thank you.' I don't hear that. I think that if we got more thank you's, we wouldn't feel so tired."

Unfortunately, there's no way to guarantee other people's reactions to your efforts. But there are two things you can do on your own to feel better. This year, you might want to concentrate more of your energy on things that you personally enjoy doing. By finding more of your rewards in the actual process of doing things, you will find yourself less dependent on other people's responses. Second, how about trying to involve more people in the preparations? It can be frustrating to be the only person who's putting effort into the celebration. And you will probably find that the rest of your family will enjoy having a more active role to play. (The next two chapters will give you some suggestions on how to include your husband and children.)

Question 2: *Sometimes I wonder who's in control of my Christmas, me or my mother. I am twenty-six and I've never celebrated the holiday in my own house, even though I have a child of my own. How can I let her know that I would like to start my own traditions without hurting her feelings?*

Answer: This question comes up surprisingly often. To get a better understanding of the problem, it might help if you look at the problem from both points of view. For decades, your mother has put large amounts of energy into her family Christmas, nurturing a set of family traditions that have become very important to her. To give this up and let her children start their own celebrations may feel like both a huge loss and an unwelcome reminder of her age.

You, however, are feeling the understandable need to create your own family Christmas. Having your own traditions and celebrating in your own house can be an important rite of passage. After all, this is a step that your own mother took years ago. Besides, your idea of how to celebrate Christmas may be quite different from your mother's and you may be eager for a chance to express it.

But Christmas is probably the time of year when you least want to rock the boat. Finding a workable solution will require tact and diplomacy and a keen awareness of the kind of relationship you have with your mother. If it is a frank, comfortable relationship, the best course of action may be to simply explain your desire to celebrate in your own home and then arrange another time during the holiday season (New Year's or Christmas Eve, for example) to spend time together, or invite her to come celebrate Christmas with you. Be sure to talk with her early enough in the year so that she can get used to the idea.

If you have reason to believe that your mother would not understand your wishes or would be too threatened by them, you may decide to compromise. You can continue to celebrate Christmas with her and then plan another celebration in your own home at a different time. This will allow you to start creating your own traditions and give you some of the independence you are looking for, but you will not have to openly confront your mother.

You may think of an even better way to solve this problem. Just keep in mind that your mother has sincere reasons for wanting to keep things the same and that your wish to create your own celebration is also natural and understandable.

Question 3: *My problem is that I don't want to give up any of my holiday activities. I enjoy them all. But I definitely get overextended. What can I do to be more relaxed?*

Answer: Many women find that by starting their holiday preparations early in the year, they can do everything they want to do and still feel relaxed. For example, one woman decided to make one gift a week starting in October. By the middle of December, they were all done and she had the peace of mind to enjoy the celebration.

But many of the women we've talked to do not like to start preparing for Christmas that early. It seems unnatural to them to be working on fruitcakes and Christmas stockings in 80-degree weather. If that's the case for you, here are two other approaches.

First, make a list of all the things that you would like to do this Christmas and arrange them in order of priority, placing the things that you absolutely have to do or most enjoy doing at the top of the list. The projects at the bottom of the list are optional, or of less importance to you.

Attack the list in order. Give yourself credit not for doing as many as possible, but for doing each project in an enjoyable fashion. Even though you may not get to the projects at the bottom of the list, you will finish most of your high-priority activities and will not feel unduly pressured.

For the second approach, you need to take a longer-range view. Each year, vow to do one or two of your favorite holiday projects. For example, this year you may decide to make a beautiful wreath for the door, as well as your own Christmas cards. The following year, you might have a neighborhood party or make some of your own gifts, without making a wreath or Christmas cards. The third year, you can do a complicated holiday baking project, making a gingerbread house with your children, but forget the other projects. This way, you will eventually get to do all that you want, but each holiday season will be more relaxed.

☆

CHAPTER 2:

Men: The Christmas Stagehands

In the fall of 1980 we gave our workshop for a group of twenty-one women at a community college in Salem, Oregon. During the morning discussion period, the women talked primarily about what their lives were like at Christmas. But after lunch, they began talking about their husbands' role in the celebration. The discussion began when one woman hesitantly volunteered: "I don't know if anyone else feels this way, but my life would be a whole lot easier at Christmas if my husband helped out more. It's a one-woman show at our house. My husband used to help wrap the presents, but now he's even dropped out of that."

As soon as she had made this comment, half a dozen other women chimed in. All six of them had husbands who did very little for Christmas. In fact, after comparing notes, they were amused to find out that each husband could be counted on to do just five fairly standard holiday chores: jotting notes on Christmas cards, putting the tree in the stand, stringing the lights, mixing drinks for company, and buying gifts for his wife ("at the last minute," added one woman). The wives did the rest of the work with little or no assistance.

All of these women wanted their husbands to help out more with the holiday chores. But after exploring this idea for a while, they realized that getting help with the workload was not the most important issue. Even more than that, they wanted their husbands to be enthusiastic about Christmas and to be more emotionally involved in the family holiday activities. This last point was especially important to them, because more than anything else they wanted Christmas to bring their families closer together, while actually it often seemed to pull them apart.

These women's problems are surprisingly common. It's often the case that men are less excited about Christmas than their wives. And women find that the season loses much of its joy when their husbands watch from the sidelines. But because they don't understand why their husbands feel cut off from the joy of Christmas in the first place, they don't know how to involve them. All they know is that the enthusiasm that comes so naturally to them is foreign to their husbands.

After two years of listening to women talk about their husbands at Christmas, we began to wonder what it would be like to hear a room full of men, not women, discussing their holiday role. Although we had always had a few men in each workshop, they were in the minority and never had a chance to explore their feelings with full male support. We decided to assemble an all-male discussion group to get a better understanding of how men really feel about Christmas.

We sent out invitations to ten thoughtful, communicative married men. In this group there were two woodworkers, an instrument maker, a construction worker, an architect, a musician, a social worker, a city planner, a truck driver, and a teacher. All but one of the men had children. Two of them had been single fathers for many years and were now remarried.

We had no idea how any of them felt about Christmas, but as we had predicted, most of them found the idea of getting together to explore their thoughts and feelings about the holiday somewhat amusing. One man exemplified the good-natured cynicism of the group when he commented: "What could men possibly have to say about Christmas? I thought it was a women's holiday."

Throughout the first half hour of the luncheon meeting, a lighthearted tone prevailed. But gradually the conversation grew more thoughtful. It became clear that Christmas meant more to the men than many women might think. Beneath their jokes and male camaraderie, they had strong, positive feelings about the holiday. They talked nostalgically about their childhood Christmases, discussed at great length the pros and cons of telling their children the truth about Santa Claus, and revealed a deep need to feel connected with family and friends at Christmastime.

When the men got down to discussing their actual family celebrations, the differences among them became more apparent. One of the men, thirty-three-year-old Paul, was quite content with his family Christmas. Newly remarried, he, like his wife, viewed Christmas as an opportunity to devote more time and energy to family activities. And to a much greater extent than the other men in the group, Paul was involved in the actual holiday preparations. "Jean doesn't get burdened with the heavy stuff," he said. "What we do, we do equally."

Twenty-eight-year-old Frank was at the other end of the spectrum. He said that he was often depressed at Christmas, and one of the reasons was that he and his wife seemed to go through the holiday on different tracks. He told the group that the previous December, his wife had stayed up sewing and baking night after night. He, on the other hand, had done his best to ignore Christmas. He had hardly given it a serious thought until December 23, and even then he had to force himself to do some last-minute shopping. "There's very little that I look forward to at Christmas," he said. "I enjoy putting up the Christmas tree. And I like to watch the kids open their gifts. But to start on a big buildup like my wife—it's just not going to happen."

Even though Frank had little enthusiasm for Christmas, he tried to hide his negative feelings from his wife. "When my wife comes running to me with her twentieth cookie recipe, I say, 'That's great.' But I'm not thinking that at all." This playacting made him feel even further removed from the festivities. He felt that Christmas was something he had to perform, and that he couldn't say what was really on his mind or do what he really wanted.

The rest of the eight men fell somewhere between these extremes. They looked forward to Christmas and were involved in some of the preparations—especially those that included their children. But overall, the reality of Christmas was often disappointing to them. The holiday seemed to escalate their financial worries, double their obligations, and frustrate their wishes for relaxed, intimate gatherings with family and friends. "What you really want to do is sit in front of the fire with your family, or call up a few friends and have them drop in. But that's the last thing you get to do," said one of the men. "Everything is packed into a tight schedule and it's always go, go, go." Much to their regret, Christmas seemed like an unwelcome interruption in the daily routine, a hurdle to surmount year after year.

From all of our conversations with men, we know that this group of men is a representative sample. Most men aren't overly upset about Christmas, but at the same time they don't find the deep enjoyment they're looking for. They look upon Christmas as a fairly enjoyable but overrated family holiday that promises more than it delivers. On a scale of 1 to 10, most men would probably give Christmas a 5.

Society gives men little encouragement to try to improve this rating. Men are expected to grumble a little about the holiday, not get too interested in the goings-on, help out when needed, and muster some enthusiasm when Christmas finally rolls around. This arm's-length attitude toward the holiday is reflected in the December issues of men's magazines. While women's magazines offer their readers a glowing vision of a wonderful Christmas, men's magazines do their best to ignore the celebration. Their only concession to the holiday is a dramatic increase in liquor ads, a photo essay on gifts for men (not what men should buy or make for other people), and the inevitable racy or cynical Christmas cartoons. The overall message to men seems to be "Drink up. The inconvenience will soon be over."

Despite this lack of encouragement, whenever we've listened to men talking at length about Christmas, they've always revealed that Christmas is very important to them. Just as much as women, they value the opportunity the holiday gives them for family togetherness, high spirits, and spiritual fulfillment, and it matters very much to them that these opportunities are realized. The men in the discussion group were no exception. As one of them summarized it, "I guess we all want Christmas to be a time of closeness and sharing. I think that is a lot of what Christ and his message are all about."

When men find that Christmas doesn't live up to its billing, it usually helps them to take a closer look at their role in the celebration. As is the case for women, men gain a better understanding of their problems when they stop to gather some data about what they actually do for the holiday.

The first thing that most men learn when they examine their Christmas responsibilities is that their holiday role is much more limited than their wives'. The typical husband provides emotional and financial support, helps out with errands, makes a handful of suggestions, and is responsible for a few well-defined parts of the celebration. If women are the Christmas Magicians, then men are the stagehands tugging the ropes.

A lot of men are fairly comfortable with the broad outlines of this role. Like their fathers before them, they expect to play a subordinate part in the celebration; and many husbands are grateful that their wives are in charge. Said one man, "I'm glad that my wife does most of the work. I could never equal her energy. I'm too laid back." But when men explore their role in greater detail, they often find that being so uninvolved is the source of some of their dissatisfaction.

One drawback is that because they're so uninvolved in the holiday preparations, it's difficult for them to build up much interest in the celebration. When they're working hard at their outside jobs right up until the day before Christmas, they can hardly be expected to jump into the festivities with a full measure of holiday joy. In addition, their limited holiday role means that only a fraction of their talents is brought to bear on the celebration. How much pride can a man take in stringing the lights and serving the drinks? As a result, men rarely get the satisfaction of a job well done that their wives feel.

Second, because women often set the overall tone of the celebration, naturally relying on their own tastes, talents, and preferences, it's fairly common for their husbands' wishes to be less well represented. One of the results is that many women perpetuate their own childhood traditions to a greater degree than their husbands'. Although men are often slow to admit that their childhood Christmas traditions have much importance to them, those early experiences can have a greater impact on their enjoyment of Christmas than they themselves realize. No less than their wives, men have fond memories of the specific activities and traditions of their childhood, and they derive great pleasure from reenacting them for themselves and their own children. If men don't have this connection to their past, the holiday can lose a lot of its emotional appeal.

This was especially true for Ken, one of the men at the luncheon. Ken had been the single parent of three children for five years. When he had remarried, his second wife assumed full responsibility for Christmas. "And I was ready for that," he said. "I welcomed her energy." But, like most women, his wife brought with her a full complement of traditions as part of her dowry. "There was no question but that we did things her way," Ken explained. He gave an example: "When I was young, we always opened our gifts on Christmas Eve. But in my wife's family, they opened them on Christmas morning. She decided that we would open ours on Christmas morning, too. There was no compromise," he said. "Except that I compromised one hundred percent." Ken said that the first year he had opened the gifts in the morning, he felt really disoriented. "It just wasn't Christmas."

There's a final problem with men playing such a limited role in the holiday. Because men often have less decision-making power at Christmas than their wives, they sometimes feel as if they are playing a walk-on part in someone else's dramatic production. Frank, the man in the group who was often depressed at Christmas, felt this the most. "My wife calls all the shots. It's always 'Go Here.' 'Go there.' And 'You *will* go there.' I have only two choices. I can go along willingly, or I can go along reluctantly."

To one degree or another, many men we've talked to have the same feeling as Frank. It seems to them that their wives' sensibilities and social lives determine the holiday events. Women make most of the decisions about which friends and relatives to see and fill in the dates on the social calendar. Although the men have veto power, when they exercise it they are cast in a negative role.

It's clear that with women in charge, men's wishes, values, and desires are often overlooked. What would Christmas be like if the male point of view were better represented? Despite their complaints, most men tell us they wouldn't make radical changes in the celebration. They just want some minor adjustments—a few more holiday activities that reflect their interests, more recognition of their important childhood traditions, and a stronger voice in the decision-making. For example, when we asked the ten men at the luncheon what their ideal Christmas would be, Frank volunteered: "I know what my perfect Christmas would be—it would be essentially like it is, only I'd set aside some time to go hunting. And the rest of it would be simpler. But the most important thing is that my wife would ask me, 'What would *you* like to do today?' Probably it would be the same kind of thing we usually do, anyway. But it would be my choice, too."

It was important for these men to develop their ideas without their wives being present. For many of them, this was the first time they had felt the freedom to explore their real feelings about Christmas. When they did, they realized that they had valid and unexpressed reasons for feeling left out. But it's clear that women need to be included in the discussion at some point. If men and women just developed separate lists of grievances, nothing would get resolved. The key to a better Christmas for husbands and wives is better communication.

One of the first things that men and women discover when they talk openly about Christmas is that they want fundamentally the same things. Despite the weight of their inherited roles and the overlay of cultural expectations, they bring basically the same needs and desires to the celebration. They want to take a break from their daily routines, to spend relaxed time with their families, and to feel connected with experiences larger than themselves. They want the comfort of familiar activities and welcome the overall structure of their traditional roles. And most men and women favor making simple and gradual changes rather than radical ones.

But most couples discover that they have some differences to resolve. For example, a husband and wife may have equally strong attachments to their childhood Christmases, they may each want a different pace in the celebration, and they may have different ideas on how much money to spend. Because Christmas is such an emotional issue for most people, it's important that they sit down and talk to each other with sensitivity and a spirit of compromise. The effort almost always bears fruit. When husbands and wives learn about each other's wishes and work toward a mutually satisfying celebration, the whole family benefits. Women get more help and support from their husbands. Men regain an emotional investment in Christmas. And children find that they have two enthusiastic parents to share the holiday with.

One couple told us how they had worked out their differences. Tom and Cathy live in a small town where he is the director of probation services and she is a part-time social service consultant.

They have two children. "In my first marriage, I felt left out of Christmas," said Tom. "I wasn't involved in the planning and I used to get pretty depressed. There were all these things I 'had to do.' I had no choice whatsoever. Marrying Cathy made all the difference. But it didn't happen automatically; we had to work on it."

One of the ways they worked at it was by listening to each other. Cathy explained, "I learned that it's important to Tom to get a lot of presents, even though it isn't to me. So now I make sure he gets lots of small, homemade gifts. And I found out that he had been depressed at Christmas for years because of money worries. So we started making all of our gifts."

Cathy and Tom have a deep respect for each other's values, and their celebration is a blend of both of their traditions. But it wasn't always that way. As Cathy told us, "I came from a family where we have a set way of doing things. It would have been really easy for me to come to this marriage with ten billion traditions of my own. In fact, I tried to do that at first, but Tom helped me see that my ready-made Christmas was not his. Now we take the good things from my family and the good things from his family and add the things we think of ourselves."

As this story shows, warm family Christmases don't spring forth in full perfection. Husbands and wives need to talk when silence would be safer, and compromise when following one set of traditions would be easier. By respecting each other's values and feelings about the holiday and finding ways to enjoy the season together, a couple can make Christmas a time of close communion.

On the following pages, there are some simple exercises for men who want to take a closer look at their feelings about Christmas, and answers to questions that men often have about the holiday.

Exercises for Men

Exercise 1: RATING YOUR ENJOYMENT OF LAST YEAR'S CHRISTMAS ACTIVITIES

1. Scan the list below and cross off the activities that you weren't involved in, adding those that we have overlooked.

- ☆ Decorating the house
- ☆ Decorating the tree
- ☆ Shopping for gifts
- ☆ Making gifts
- ☆ Wrapping gifts
- ☆ Entertaining
- ☆ Going to parties
- ☆ Going to Christmas performances
- ☆ Christmas activities with your children
- ☆ Christmas activities at work
- ☆ Religious activities at home
- ☆ Church activities
- ☆ Gift-opening rituals
- ☆ Charitable activities
- ☆ Family Christmas gathering
- ☆ Music
- ☆ Other

2. Beside each of the remaining activities, assign a number from 1 to 10 that shows how much you enjoyed doing it last year. A 10 shows the most pleasure. Feel free to add comments.

3. Think about what, overall, gave you the greatest pleasure last Christmas.

4. Which activities or situations gave you the least pleasure?

Exercise 2: REMEMBERING YOUR CHILDHOOD CHRISTMAS

1. Think back to your childhood Christmas. Which traditions, activities, or occasions were particularly pleasurable for you?

2. Of these important childhood memories, which of them are reflected in your current celebration?

Exercise 3: AN EXERCISE FOR MARRIED MEN—YOUR ROLE IN YOUR CURRENT CELEBRATION

1. Which of the following statements most accurately reflects your role in your celebration?

a. My wife determines nearly all of the holiday events.
b. My wife determines more of the holiday events than I do.
c. We share the planning fifty-fifty.
d. My influence predominates.

2. How do you feel about this arrangement?

Exercise 4: DRAWING CONCLUSIONS

1. From everything you know about yourself and Christmas, ideally, what changes would you like to make in the coming celebration? (For the moment, don't take into consideration how realistic or unrealistic these changes may be.)

2. For married men: What do you most want your wife to know about how you feel about Christmas?

Two men who completed this exercise shared their answers with us. Steve, a thirty-seven-year-old business executive and the father of two young girls, rated his enjoyment of the previous Christmas and discovered that the activities he had enjoyed most involved his children and making gifts for other people. And the first exercise helped him realize how angry he was at all the encroaching materialism. "I feel I have to ward off the world and protect my children from the cheapening effects of commercialism."

When Steve thought about his childhood Christmas he realized that he had a wealth of happy memories. Among other things, he liked "bubble-lights on the trees," celebrating a Swedish tradition called Little Christmas on the night before Christmas, and his mother's decorating the windows with stencils.

When he thought about it, very few of his treasured traditions were being enacted in his current celebration; for example, he now opened his gifts on Christmas morning instead of Christmas Eve. The changes he wanted to make were to have more Advent rituals at home ("I like to get revved up over a long period of time"), to have more religious content in the family celebration, and to find ways of shutting out holiday commercialism. The one thing he wanted his wife to do differently was to be more sensitive to the way his family celebrated Christmas.

Arnold, a thirty-one-year-old woodworker and the father of a teen-age daughter and a five-year-old son, realized that the most important thing about Christmas to him was spending relaxed time with his own family and getting together with his parents. The thing he liked least was the fact that the whole country had blown Christmas out of proportion ("It should be simple, you know") and that his own celebration seemed too tense and rushed. "I'd like to wade into Christmas Eve feeling halfway calm," he said.

His important memories of his childhood centered not so much on specific activities but on the whole aura of relaxed calm that his family had cultivated at Christmas. "There was no pressure. There was no worrying about money. It was simple and under control."

Arnold was often depressed by the frantic pace of Christmas, and wanted very much to scale things down and for his wife to be less busy. He wanted her to take on only projects that she could do comfortably. And he wished that he had more time off from work to take part in the Christmas activities in a leisurely fashion.

In the remaining chapters of this book, men will have a chance to explore other aspects of Christmas and to clarify any changes they might want to make in the celebration.

Questions and Answers

Question 1: *I don't think I've been genuinely happy at Christmas since I was a child. What's wrong?*

Answer: Some time during the transition from childhood to full adulthood, Christmas begins to change for people. The magic and surprise and beauty of Christmas are tempered by all the careful thought and work and expense that they put into the happiness of others. For many people this transition is accelerated by the birth of their own children. At that point they step over the line separating the Christmas recipients from the Christmas providers.

But even given this inevitable change in feelings, you can still find a deeper and more mature satisfaction in the holiday. The first thing you need to do is to accept the fact that, as an adult, you will rarely experience Christmas in the same way you did as a child. When you let go of that universal desire to be young at Christmas, you will make room for the new kind of pleasure you can find as an adult.

Also, as we said in the body of this chapter, you will probably find that your enjoyment of Christmas is increased if you carry over some traditions from your childhood into your current celebration. You won't feel exactly the same way about them as you did when you were young, but your Christmas will be enriched by the memories of all those that have gone before.

Finally, reading this chapter and doing the exercises have probably given you some important information about other ways to increase your enjoyment of Christmas. We have talked with men who have gone from being depressed at Christmas to finding it one of the most enjoyable parts of the year. They did this by actively seeking a new role that matches their personalities and beliefs.

Question 2: *How can I enjoy Christmas when I'm so busy at work that I hardly have time to turn around?*

Answer: If you have the luxury, take a few days off from work at Christmas. One man that we talked to had had to take a week off one Christmas because his office shut down to do some remodeling. He enjoyed Christmas so much more that year that he has taken a vacation at the end of December ever since.

If taking time off at Christmas isn't practical, even a few unscheduled hours of leisure time can restore your spirits and replenish your energy for the things you want to do for the holiday. You might want to cancel your usual meetings or delay activities you generally enjoy—bridge games, bowling, night classes—until January.

Finally, you may want to eliminate some of your usual holiday activities. Many men find that they would rather give up a tradition than do it in a rushed, frantic way. By scaling down your obligations, you will have more time and peace of mind to enjoy the ones that remain. (Later chapters will help you simplify your celebration.)

Question 3: *My wife and I often fight over money at Christmas. What should we do?*

Answer: Both men and women are placed in awkward positions at Christmas. Men are given the message that their success as husbands and fathers depends on how much money they make available for the family Christmas. But on the other hand, they are typically excluded from many of the actual decisions about how that money is spent. In most cases, their wives are the ones who choose the gifts and write the checks. Men are often left out of this process until they are presented with the final bill. Understandably, many men are upset by the fact that their primary function is to provide the funds and that they have so little control over how they're spent.

Women may not only be contributing to the family income, but also carrying most of the responsibility for deciding how the money should be spent. They are the ones who have to make sure that Aunt Hattie has her customary gift, that the dinner lives up to everyone's expectations (her husband's included), and that the children are suitably outfitted for the Holiday Review at Grandma's. And women are often the only ones in their families who fully realize how much these things cost. When their husbands open the bills, the men are often unaware of all the careful planning and bargain-hunting that went into keeping the totals as low as they are. All they see is that Christmas costs way too much.

Understanding this double bind is the first step in resolving the problem. Even when a couple chooses to keep the traditional financial arrangement, they profit from consulting each other more frequently during the holiday season so that both of them are aware of the total monetary picture.

But poor communication is not the only source of financial tension at Christmas. More and more people are coming to the conclusion that they are simply spending too much money. No matter who's making the decisions and who's making the money, spending can get out of hand. In every chapter of this book you will find specific suggestions for trimming your expenses.

In addition to adjusting the total amount of money they are spending, many people see the need for more conscious financial planning at Christmas. They want to know ahead of time how much money they have available and ensure that that money is spent on things they value. A simple holiday budget plan that may help can be found in the Appendix.

Question 4: *Every Christmas I feel a little down. How can I keep from being so depressed?*

Answer: Dr. Calvin Frederick, formerly of the National Institute of Mental Health, estimates that there is a 15 percent increase in the number of people seeking professional help for depression in the period surrounding Christmas. Like you, a lot of people go through the holiday season feeling sad and unhappy just when they want to feel their best.

There may be any number of reasons for your unhappiness. You may have family problems. You may be worried about money. You may have health problems or job concerns. Or you may be lonely. Unfortunately, problems don't disappear at Christmas, and many people find that they are intensified. We want so much to be lighthearted and gay that the bad moods we can cope with at other times of the year seem unmanageable during the holiday season.

Some people find that their depression feeds on itself. In the beginning, they are unhappy for a specific reason. Then they are upset at themselves for being unhappy at Christmas. And they may also resent the real or imagined pressure from those around them to be in a better mood. All of this can turn a mild case of the blues into a black mood.

Dr. Frederick suggests several things you can do that might help you raise your spirits. First, stop putting unreasonable pressure on yourself to be happy at Christmas. Despite appearances, most people are no more or less happy at Christmas than at any other time of the year. And when you have legitimate reasons for being unhappy, acknowledge them.

Second, you may find that your bad mood improves when you're in the company of special friends and favorite relatives—especially those who accept your full range of feelings and don't put pressure on you to be other than you are. So seek out people who make you feel better, and avoid people who contribute to your depression.

Third, make an effort to be more physically active. Physical activity is one of the best antidotes to depression. Recent research indicates that exercise stimulates the production of endorphins, mood-elevating chemicals produced by the body. Take a walk, go to the gym, get out in the country, or take on a project that calls for physical activity.

Fourth, many people recover their equilibrium when they set one or two specific, manageable goals every day—even if they are as simple as cleaning out a closet or writing a letter. The satisfaction they get from completing these tasks adds to their sense of well-being and self-respect.

Finally, watch your intake of alcohol. While a few drinks will make you feel temporarily euphoric, alcohol is a depressant and often ends up making you feel worse than before.

Note: If you are feeling seriously depressed (that is, if you have trouble sleeping, have lost your appetite, have thoughts of suicide, or feel hopeless) you should seek professional help.

☆

CHAPTER 3:

The Four Things Children Really Want for Christmas

Deborah, a twenty-nine-year-old homemaker, lives with her husband and their son, Alex, in a trailer in the backwoods of western Oregon. Deborah told us that her most memorable Christmas had been the year before, when Alex was three. Despite the fact that she had had very little money to spend on gifts, spent the entire week before Christmas in bed with the flu, and had to cancel all visits with her friends and family because of her illness, it had been a wonderful Christmas. She told us that Alex had made all the difference. "He was the perfect age to be excited about Christmas," she said. "It took so little to please him. His favorite gift of all was a one-dollar race car he found in his stocking." She said that for the first time since she was a child, she had felt real joy at Christmas.

When the two of us became parents, we, too, were more excited about the holiday than we had been in years. We found that we looked forward to Christmas morning with the same eagerness we had felt twenty-five years earlier, only this time we were excited about the gifts our children would unwrap, not about anything we would receive. And our children gave us a wonderful excuse to bring out the forgotten artifacts of our childhood—the Advent calendars, Christmas books, and angel chimes. Being the parents of young children gave us back some of the lost magic of Christmas.

In addition to these simple joys, our children gave us a welcome incentive to stop and examine our holiday activities. We realized that an appraisal of how we celebrated Christmas was long overdue. And when we took a look at what we did, we discovered that the spontaneous approach to Christmas that had worked when we were childless—one year at this parent's, one year at that parent's, and maybe a third year spent with friends—seemed a little haphazard. We had newfound energy for creating a more enduring celebration.

Most of the parents who come to our workshops have this same desire for strong, family-centered traditions and they're eager for suggestions on how to give their children a wonderful Christmas. But some parents come with specific problems as well, because in addition to the joy children bring to Christmas, they can also bring added concerns. The problem we hear about most often from parents is that their children seem overly preoccupied with gifts. As early as the age of four or five, children may lose the ability to be delighted by the sights and sounds of Christmas, only to gain a two-month-long obsession with expensive toys. Suddenly all they seem to care about is how many presents they will be getting and how many days are left until they can open them.

We've run across this problem in every workshop we have ever given, but one woman's story stands out. Shelley, the mother of a nine-year-old boy named John, came to a workshop we gave in 1981 because she had found the following letter to Santa in her son's bedroom. In a schoolboy's scrawl, John had asked Santa for dozens of presents, most of them name-brand toys.

Shelley didn't think she was contributing to John's unrealistic expectations. "Gifts are an insignificant part of Christmas to me," she said. "When I was young I never would have had the nerve to sit down and copy out a whole toy catalog." She believed that John was picking up his gift mania from things around him—his friends, television commercials, and store displays. Everything seemed to conspire to make him greedy, and she felt powerless to ward off all the outside influences. All she could do was feel disappointed in her inability to teach John better values.

Like Shelley, many parents find it difficult to create a simple, value-centered family Christmas in the midst of all the commercial pressures today. But despite their feelings of helplessness, parents can determine the quality of the celebration. In order to do this, they need to learn what it is that all children really want for Christmas.

While most children are quick to tell their parents that what they want for Christmas are video games, Strawberry Shortcake dolls, *Star Wars* toys, and makeup kits, they have more fundamental needs than this. From talking with children, parents, and child specialists, we've learned that in addition to a few well-chosen gifts, children really want and need four basic things for Christmas:

1. Relaxed and loving time with the family
2. Realistic expectations about gifts
3. An evenly paced holiday season
4. Strong family traditions

These four unspoken needs play the determining role in whether or not children have a good family Christmas. In the rest of this chapter, we'll explore them one by one.

The first requirement on this list, relaxed and loving time with the family, will come as no surprise to most parents. They are aware that, even more than gifts, children want love at Christmas. Dr. Milton Levine, a respected child specialist and professor emeritus at Cornell University, agrees. "The greatest need of all children at Christmas—just like at any time of the year—is the assurance that they are very much wanted and loved by their parents."

33. Saturday Night Fever Record
34. Coloring Book
35. Elecktric Battleship
36. Super tuber
37. Intercept
38. AM Speedsteer
39. BeBe gun
40. HakinSpace
41. Maxmachine NightHawk
42. [crossed out]
43. Shasam Underoos
44. StrateGo
45. Glow in the dark shrinkidinks
46. Increadable Hulk instant muscle's
47. Energise Spiderman set
48. Downfall
49. Slapsie
50. Layan egg game
51. Knockout game
52. Bowling Ball
53. Skidoo
53. Superstar 3000
54. Sit and spin
55. Suckerman
56. ROM
57. walk and talking race pack
58. Hit and missle
59. Ranger TV
60. Hot weels
61. Torture chamber
62. Drum set
63. Attack!

Dear Santa Please Bring me

1. Danvan
2. Race and chace
3. Roket
4. Spidermanset
5. Crayons
6. CowBoy suit and hat and Boots, gun
7. Fishing pole
8. Clothes-size-7 shirt
9. Big Deteour Racetrack
10. Dead Stopgame
11. match Box Garage
12. Bigtrack
13. miky mouse clock
14. eingtine game
15. the american Dream game
16. Teddy Bear
17. Lunch Box
18. Coat
19. Radio
20. Socer Ball
21. mouse trap game
22. Big ectgo
23. Foot Ball
24. hangman
25. Spiderman
26. Tavoy Brown record
27. major merga
28. crash up derby
29. star trek mica
30. Pro Thunder Bike
31. Alien monster

But the problem is, many parents who do a good job of making their children feel loved and wanted the other eleven months of the year fall short in December. Shelley, the mother of the boy with the long gift list, was a prime example. At first, she couldn't see how anything she was doing fostered her son's obsession with gifts. But she gained more insight into John's problem when we asked her to tell us what their family life was like in the weeks before Christmas. Shelley said that she worked full-time as a seamstress in a swimsuit factory, and in December the few hours she had off were crowded with holiday chores. John's father was also busier than usual because he was a salesman in a sporting goods store, and the store made as much as a third of its annual sales between Thanksgiving and Christmas. As a result, the family had very little relaxed time together. Shelley began to see that one of the reasons John spent so much time daydreaming about gifts was that they spent so little time together as a family.

This is an all-too-common problem. Parents are often away from their children more in December than in any other month of the year, as their lives become crowded with church rehearsals, benefits, shopping trips, parties, concerts, or social events. And when they're at home, they are often preoccupied with holiday chores, Christmas plans, and money worries. This constant busyness can make December a lonely month for children. Even though they are showered with gifts and affection on the twenty-fourth and twenty-fifth of December, this two-day burst of attention is rarely enough. Children want love in a steady, constant way.

To give children this even, uninterrupted attention, most parents need to set firm priorities. When they make a conscious decision to set aside some relaxed time to be with their families, their children get the most important gift of all, their undivided attention. Often this involves some sacrifice. We talked with a couple from Colorado who found the only way they could spend a good deal of time with their children was to turn down all social invitations after mid-December. Another woman told us that Christmas had gotten so hectic she had to tell her relatives that her family wouldn't be traveling for Christmas, even though she risked offending them. Both of these families had made time with their children their top priority and felt well rewarded by their children's deep enjoyment of Christmas.

The second thing that children need at Christmas is a balanced attitude toward gifts. On the surface, children seem to enjoy being preoccupied with Christmas presents. But any parent who has watched a child plow through a huge stack of gifts on Christmas morning, and then look around the room as if he's lost his best friend, knows that this isn't true. When all of their excitement about Christmas is focused on gifts alone, children feel terribly let down, because as marvelous as the new games and toys may be, they can't possibly live up to all those weeks of breathless anticipation. Children need to spread out their excitement about Christmas to other parts of the celebration as well.

But many parents feel stymied in their efforts to place gifts in their proper perspective by the incessant holiday advertising. Watching television on a typical Saturday morning in December, a child may see from fifty to sixty toy commercials using the most sophisticated techniques Madison Avenue has at its disposal. And as any parent knows, those ads are amazingly effective. One father told us about one time when his six-year-old son was watching a commercial for a popular board game. When it was over, his son turned to him and said, "I want that game for Christmas." The father explained to us that there was nothing remarkable in the fact that his son had asked for a toy that had just been advertised. He did that all the time. But this case was different. "We had that game already," said the father, "and my son was bored to tears with it. The commercial sold him on something he already owned."

Children are one of the prime targets of the Christmas Machine, because toys are the most dependable part of the holiday trade. No matter how little money people have, they will always find a way to buy toys for their children. And advertisers learned long ago that it is more effective to target their toy commercials at children than at the parents who ultimately do the buying. The following comments are from an article in an advertising trade journal titled *Advertising Age* (July 19, 1965): "When you sell a woman on a product and she goes into the store and finds your brand isn't in stock, she'll probably forget it. But when you sell a kid on your product, if he can't get it, he will throw himself on the floor, stamp his feet, and cry. You can't get a reaction like that from an adult."

What can parents do about all the toy commercials? First, they need to know that no matter how influential the toy commercials may be, their own influence is many times stronger. Children want and need to have their parents define the celebration for them. When parents take the time to talk with their children about gifts, share with them their own sense of values, and, most important, back up those words with a family celebration of which gifts form only one part, children quickly learn that there's more fun to Christmas than just unwrapping packages. When children have exciting family activities to look forward to before and after the present-opening, gifts start taking their rightful place in the festivities.

Second, parents may want to arm their youngest children with extra defenses against the ads. Studies have shown that the younger the child, the more he or she is influenced by television commercials. For example, children five and younger often can't distinguish between commercials and regular programming, and many children as old as nine or ten can't readily explain the purpose of advertising.

An easy way for parents to turn their young children into more sophisticated viewers is to watch an hour of children's television with them and have them say, "Commercial!" each time a new one comes on the screen. Then talk about each one. What is being advertised? How are the products made to look especially inviting? Children will quickly learn to distinguish commercials from regular programming and will begin to get more insight into the function of advertising. We've talked with children as young as four years of age who knew that the purpose of advertising is to sell things, and that commercials can make toys appear more exciting than they really are.

But manipulative toy advertising is not the only part of the merchant's Christmas that can have a negative effect on children. Another disruptive influence is the way the needs of retailers have distorted the natural rhythm of the holiday season. This aspect of holiday commercialism is not so obvious, but it still has a dramatic effect on children. To understand how commercialism has rearranged the traditional holiday season, it's important to get a sense of how the season was paced a hundred years ago.

In the 1880s, there was a much shorter buildup to Christmas because retail stores did not have such an overwhelming investment in holiday sales. It wasn't until mid-December that holiday decorations began appearing in city streets and stores. But today, stores start gearing up for Christmas in late October or early November because of their need to have as long a shopping season as possible. And, as any parent knows, as soon as a child sees the first cardboard Santa in a variety store, the long countdown to Christmas begins. Children today may have a ninety-day wait for Christmas.

Even while the buildup to Christmas has been lengthened, its ending has been cut short. For example, a hundred years ago the festivities continued on through New Year's. There were Christmas dances, family games, and holiday traditions that kept Christmas alive for at least a week. Today, the commercial interests pack up their special decorations, Santas, and holiday music on December 26 because there's no more chance to sell. And families who link the Christmas calendar to the commercial celebration often have nothing to offer their children after December

25, either. When the gifts have been unwrapped, Christmas is over and children are left dazed and bewildered. One mother told us that she found her daughter crying in the closet on Christmas Day—just after she had opened all the gifts she had asked for. When her mother asked what the matter was, the girl answered, "If I had known this was all there was to Christmas, I wouldn't have waited so long."

We made it a point to talk with young children to get more of their perspective on the holiday season. Judith, a seven-year-old girl from Los Angeles, turned out to be an eloquent spokesperson for her age group. "I have to wait two billion years for Christmas," she said. "When it comes, it only lasts a second. Then the whole world is plain again." Being a resourceful child, Judith decided to take matters into her own hands. She confided to us that she had written a secret letter to Santa, asking him to "take an early run to my house. About November 10." Then she told her parents that Santa had agreed. "I went a little too far with that one," she confessed.

It's easier than most parents think to give their children a more natural holiday season. All they have to do is hold off on their important family traditions until a week or so before Christmas, and then reserve a few favorite activities for after the twenty-fifth. Here's how one couple does this. Every year, on December 10, they celebrate the beginning of Christmas by getting out their Christmas records. On the fifteenth, they put a wreath on the front door. On December 20, they put up the tree. And on January 1, they wind down the celebration with a traditional potluck dinner for their friends and their children. The children are so secure in this order of things that they have no difficulty with the premature holiday displays. In fact, the father told us that when he was in the grocery store one day in early November with his daughters, the girls saw the manager hanging some plastic holly over the cash registers. In a loud voice the youngest girl piped up: "What's he doing that for? Doesn't he know Christmas is a long way away?"

There's a final need children have at Christmas, and that's to have a celebration enriched with family traditions. Many parents underestimate how important traditions are to their children and how many valuable purposes they serve. First of all, traditions give children the opportunity to do something they enjoy year after year. This is of great significance to children. One mother told us that for several years she and her boys had made a gingerbread house each Christmas. One year she suggested that they make a permanant one instead. But her boys would have no part of it. To them, it just wasn't Christmas if they couldn't make a gingerbread house every year.

Traditions also give children great comfort and security. When everything in their lives seems disrupted by the holiday season—school is out, their parents are extra-busy, and everyday rituals fall by the wayside—children like to have well-defined holiday traditions to hold on to. Traditions let them know exactly how the season will unfold and bring back memories of all the Christmases that have gone before.

Although such traditions are very important to children, parents don't have to run to the library and check out books on holiday customs, or struggle to invent elaborate new rituals. Very simple activities can satisfy the need for tradition. For example, one family has this custom: the first person up on December 25 puts a special Christmas record on the stereo and cracks a bowl of nuts for the rest of the family. This simple ritual heralds to the whole family that yes, indeed, this is Christmas Day.

Children perceive anything they can count on year after year as a tradition, and most families have more of these hidden rituals than they realize. The holiday food they eat every year, the customary visits they make to family and friends, the familiar decorations, the records and books that come out each December, the way the family displays its Christmas cards—all of these things enrich the children's celebration. All most parents need to do is talk with their children to find out which holiday activities are most important to them, and make an effort to do them each

Christmas. Parents may also find out that some of their holiday activities aren't as important to their children as they had thought. A family may wish to trim these extraneous traditions so that there is room for favorite ones to flourish.

Once parents, grandparents, aunts, and uncles understand what children really want for Christmas—relaxed time with their families, realistic expectations about gifts, a natural holiday season, and reliable family traditions—*and* realize how easy it is to give them these things, they can create joyful and enduring celebrations. The following pages contain an exercise that will help you help your children enjoy Christmas, answers specific questions parents have about their children, and some practical advice on how to convey important values to young children. Suggestions for good gifts for children appear in the Appendix in the back of the book.

Exercise

HELPING CHILDREN ENJOY CHRISTMAS

1. Of all the needs of children at Christmas, enjoyable time with their families is most important. Think back to last December. *Excluding* Christmas Eve and Christmas Day, did you spend (underline the correct word) more, about the same, or less happy, relaxed time with your children in December, compared to other months?

2. If your answer to the above question was "less," look through the following list and check the suggestions on how to spend more time with your children that seem most feasible for you.

- ☆ Taking extra time off from work
- ☆ Simplifying our holiday preparations
- ☆ Entertaining less
- ☆ Attending fewer parties that are just for adults

☆ Being more relaxed about how the house looks
☆ Cutting back on outside commitments
☆ Making fewer gifts
☆ Watching less television
☆ Traveling less
☆ Seeing fewer friends and relatives
☆ Other

3. Which holiday traditions do your children seem to enjoy most? (If you are uncertain, take some time in the next few days to talk with them.)

4. What holiday traditions or family activities do your children have to look forward to after December 25? (If you have none or very few, see Question 11 for some suggestions.)

5. Check the statement that most accurately completes this thought: Gift-giving plays the following role in our family celebration:

☆ It is by far the most important tradition.
☆ It is one of several important traditions.
☆ It is of moderate importance.
☆ It is of relatively minor importance.

6. On a sheet of paper, write each of your children's names and jot down a few sentences that describe his or her attitude toward Christmas presents last year. (If one or more of your children seemed overly concerned with gifts, you may wish to review this chapter.)

QUESTIONS AND ANSWERS

Question 1: *What are some ways my young children and I can have a good time together this holiday season?*

Answer: One of the easiest and most rewarding things you can do is to take a look at your existing holiday activities and see if your children have an active role to play in them. All too often at Christmas, children are the passive recipients of their parents' labors. Then, make sure that you are in a relaxed, accepting frame of mind as you take part in seasonal activities. A common tendency is for the look of the finished product to become more important than the act of creating it. One mother told us that she had a wonderful time baking cookies with her children and doing craft projects at every time of year except Christmas. Then, suddenly, she became preoccupied with making *beautiful* cookies and *beautiful* ornaments, so her children were just in the way.

One mother had a refreshingly different point of view: "I let the kids decorate the cookies with me last year with the frosting that comes in tubes. And you'd better believe those cookies had FROSTING. They looked terrible. They tasted terrible. But they were great."

To help eliminate any tension in your baking sessions, you might want to save your complicated recipes for times when the kids aren't around. You could use store-bought refrigerator cookie dough and let the kids decorate the slices with red and green sprinkles or icing from tubes. Or, if you want to make your goodies from scratch, here are two recipes that are simple enough for preschoolers.

Apricot Nut Balls

1 cup chopped apricots (1 6-ounce package)
½ cup dried coconut
½ cup graham cracker crumbs (3 to 4 double crackers)
1 to 2 tablespoons sweetened condensed milk (not evaporated)
½ cup chopped nuts

Put everything but the nuts into a bowl. Mix with a spoon. Shape into balls, logs, or cookies. Roll in the chopped nuts. Refrigerate until served.

Here is a simple no-bake fruitcake that uses dried fruit in place of candied fruit.

No-Bake Fruitcake

2 cups graham cracker crumbs (14 double crackers)
1 cup chopped nuts (you can buy them chopped)
1¼ cups chopped, mixed dried fruit (1 6-ounce package; also available chopped)
1 14-ounce can sweetened condensed milk (not evaporated)

Put all the dry ingredients into a bowl. Mix with your hands or a spoon. Add the condensed milk and stir. Line a bread pan with plastic wrap or waxed paper. Press the dough into the pan. Cover with paper and press again. Refrigerate. Then slice and serve.

Making salt-dough ornaments is another wonderful holiday activity for children, because they can mold and shape the clay to their heart's content and then, when it's dry, have the additional fun of painting it. Here's a good recipe. The ingredients are inexpensive and you probably have everything you need without making a special trip to the store.

Baker's Clay

2 cups white flour
1 cup salt
1 cup water (warm water feels good to the hands)
2 tablespoons oil

Combine all the ingredients. Knead for 10 minutes or until smooth. (If the dough is too crumbly, add water. If it's too moist, add flour.) Roll and cut with cookie cutters or shape into snow-people, gingerbread men, or whatever. Bake in a 325-degree oven until dried, but not browned (about 15 minutes per ¼ inch). When cool, paint with watercolors, acrylic paint, or felt pens. Spray with plastic for a more durable, shinier surface.

Note: If you want to hang these ornaments on the tree, insert a bent paper clip through the top before baking them.

Sprinkled throughout the rest of this chapter and in the others as well, you will find more easy projects and activities to do with your children. But the crucial element in all of them is a relaxed and accepting parent.

Question 2: *I feel that our Christmas celebration lacks meaningful traditions. How can we find good ones to add?*

Answer: Whether yours is a young family just beginning to create its own holiday traditions or a more established family that wants to add some new ones, the first place we suggest you look is in your own childhood memories. Try to recall a few significant Christmases and remember which events or activities gave you the most pleasure. How many of those traditions are included in your current celebration? If you are married, have your spouse do the same thing. You and your children will get added pleasure from knowing that your traditions have a history.

Another place you might want to look for traditions is in your parents' or grandparents' childhood Christmases. Sit down with them and have them tell you about their early holiday memories. The joy of reaching into the past and rescuing a forgotten tradition can illuminate the lives of every generation in your family.

Beyond that, you might wish to explore your ethnic heritage. Many of our most vital folk traditions are being slowly extinguished in favor of more homogeneous, commercialized activities. There are dozens of books in your public library to aid you in your research. Or, once again, call on your oldest surviving family members.

Remember that your holiday traditions can be quite simple. One family we know has made a tradition out of opening their Christmas cards. Each day, the unopened cards are placed in the center of the Advent wreath. After dinner, all three children choose cards to open. They look carefully at the illustrations, pass them around the table, and then listen while their parents read the messages inside and tell them a little about the people who sent them. This is one of the favorite traditions of all the family members, and it costs nothing, involves no preparation time, and teaches the children a little about the special people in their lives.

Question 3: *The toy commercials on television really bother me. What else can I do to protect my children from them?*

Answer: One thing you can do is become more knowledgeable about what effect television advertising and television in general have on your children. Here's a good book for more information: *The ACT Guide to Children's Television: How to Treat TV with TLC* by Evelyn Kaye (Boston: Beacon Press, 1979).

Second, you can limit your children's television viewing hours. Action for Children's Television (ACT), a nationwide organization dedicated to improving the quality of children's television, will send you a TV Time Chart that is an entertaining way for your children to monitor their own TV viewing hours. The chart rewards children for keeping their TV time between zero and ten hours per week. Send two dollars to ACT, 46 Austin Street, Newtonville, MA 02160. If you would like more information about this hard-working and effective organization, include an extra dollar for an information packet.

Question 4: *I'd like to give my children fewer gifts than I have in the past, but I'm afraid of disappointing them. What should I do?*

Answer: Many parents whom we've talked with want to reduce the importance of gifts in the family celebration. One mother told us that she used to give her teen-age children expensive gifts, like stereos and the best ski equipment. "I wanted my kids to know that they were the most important thing in the world to me," she explained. "But the only message they got was that 'Mother spent a lot of money.' I'm not going to do that anymore."

Cutting down on gifts will probably be easier than you thought. Remember that what your children really want for Christmas is a warm and close family celebration and a few carefully chosen gifts from people who care about them. The winners in the long run are not the children who get the most gifts, but the ones who have parents with strong, positive values and the courage to live by them.

Here are some suggestions to help you ease into a less present-centered celebration. First, talk to your children as soon as possible about your plans to give them fewer presents. Be clear about what they can expect. Second, explain to children who are old enough to understand why it's important to you to minimize gifts. Finally, give your children something else to look forward to, like a special trip or family activity. Focus on what they *will* be getting, not on what they won't.

Question 5: *Is it important to get my daughter the one thing she really wants? She's only three and a half and she wants a Barbie doll.*

Answer: Most of the child specialists we've talked with agree that getting your child that one thing that's at the top of her list helps her see that you are paying close attention to her wishes and dreams, even though—and this is the tricky part—you may not fully support them. But on the other hand, if you have *strong* objections to your children's requests, it's better to be honest and help them think of other things they'd like equally well. When older children ask for gifts that are too expensive, for example, it's better to say quite honestly, "That sounds like a great gift, but we can't afford it this year," than to give the gift along with the hidden message that you regret spending so much money on them.

Question 6: *My parents give my children far too many gifts. We only give them a few, but the total haul is way too much. How can I ask them to give fewer gifts without hurting their feelings?*

Answer: When each well-meaning grandmother, grandfather, aunt, and uncle adds three or four gifts to the collection, children may have to spend hours opening them. And it's clear to everyone watching that a fraction of that number would be ultimately more satisfying. Quite a few of the parents we've talked with have found solutions to this problem; here are two of them:

> Last year my mother asked us what our three-year-old wanted for Christmas. In the past she had given Melissa four or five presents. We suggested that Mother spend a day with her instead, because spending time with Grandma was the best present of all. So Melissa had a wonderful day at the zoo with her grandmother and grandfather while my wife and I had a free day together to work on Christmas gifts. It was perfect.
>
> Two years ago we asked people to send us family gifts at Christmas and save individual presents for the kids' birthdays. It works beautifully. Now the boys get one present apiece from us, one from Santa, and then games and books the whole fam-

ily enjoys from everyone else. It takes the focus off each one of us and puts it on the family.

Question 7: *I don't feel comfortable telling other people how many gifts to give my children. Is there any other way to keep the total number of gifts under control?*

Answer: Again, we turn to some wise parents for their solutions.

> When relatives bring Christmas presents we let our children open them right away instead of letting them pile up until Christmas Day. Then the person who brought them gets to see their reaction. And if a present comes in the mail, we try to find a picture of the person who sent it to show to the kids as they're opening the package. They used to think the gifts came from the mailman.

> When Michael was three years old, he was given over thirty presents for Christmas. We kept most of them stored away and brought them out one at a time later in the year. He still had ten presents to open on Christmas morning, which was more than enough.

Question 8: *How can I encourage my children to be more generous at Christmas? All they seem to think about is themselves.*

Answer: Probably the best way to encourage generosity in your children at Christmas is to set a good example yourself. For example, let your children see how much fun you have giving gifts to other people. If you regularly make charitable donations at Christmas, tell them about it, and include their names in the gift. And make a special effort to give generously of your love and attention during the holiday season.

To more directly involve your children in being generous, you may wish to add special "giving" traditions to your celebration.

That way, each holiday season teaches them more about the true meaning of Christmas. But be sure to make these projects fun for the children, and don't force the issue. A child's awareness of and concern for other people develops gradually over the years—and the most potent lessons come just from watching you.

Here are some ways other families around the country have set the stage for generosity:

> In our family, my sisters and I become "secret friends" each Christmas. We draw names from a Christmas stocking and do neat things for that person, like washing dishes or helping find something that's lost. On Christmas Eve we exchange cards saying whose secret friend we've been.

> We tell our four- and two-year-olds that Santa Claus not only brings gifts, but takes gifts that have been left for him under the tree to give to needy children. Last year our four-year-old son decided to leave his favorite truck for Santa, and he seemed to feel especially good about that.

> Every Christmas I set aside a special day to take my daughter Christmas shopping to help me choose gifts for her cousins. We make it a leisurely day, go to a special restaurant for lunch, and talk about her cousins and what they would like. She comes up with wonderful ideas—things I never would have thought of.

> My kids are really extraordinary in the amount of time and thought they give each other at Christmas. We've encouraged that by giving the kids a certain amount of money to buy gifts for their brothers and sisters, and the only rule is they have to cover everybody. By the time they are eight or nine, they see Christmas as a time to show each other they really do understand who they are, what they like, and what would make them happy.

Once a year I take my children grocery-shopping and we fill up a sack with Christmas goodies—dates, candied fruit, nuts, butter, brown sugar, honey, all those expensive ingredients you have to buy at Christmastime—and then we leave them off at the Loaves and Fishes center to be given to a needy family.

Question 9: *How can I help my young children realize that Christmas is Jesus' birthday, not their own?*

Answer: If yours is a Christian family, celebrating the birth of Jesus may be the primary source of your holiday joy, and while you may take part in Christmas activities at church, you also want to bring those spiritual insights home. Here are ways that other families have helped their children celebrate Jesus' birthday.

> We hang eight stockings by the mantel, one for each of our seven children and one for Jesus. All of the kids write cards to put in Jesus' stocking, telling Him how they want to be next year.
>
> We have a birthday party for Jesus. This is the family tradition that our children look forward to most of all.
>
> In our family we bring out pieces of our family crèche a few at a time to correspond with the Christmas story. The week before Christmas, we bring out the stable, Joseph and Mary, and the animals, and let the children play with them. Every time I turn around they are in a different arrangement. On Christmas morning I bring out the Baby Jesus. And the wise men make their first appearance on Epiphany. This helps my children reenact the birth of Jesus and adds an element of drama to the crèche that it wouldn't have otherwise.
>
> When our children were very young, we read them Luke after they opened their presents, and let them dress up with scarves, robes, and jewelry to playact the story of Jesus' birth.

The Gift of Time by Margaret E. Miller, Rev. Robert Miller, Loretta Vanderveen, and Carl Vanderveen (Wilton, Conn.: Morehouse-Barlow Company, 1977) is a resource book for Christian families "designed to bring into focus the true meaning of the Advent, Christmas, and Epiphany seasons and their relevance to family life." Through crafts, prayer, and simple skits, this book helps you make the entire holiday a spiritual experience for your family.

Question 10: *How can I help my children see that Christmas is a time of goodwill toward all people on earth?*

Answer: Mankind's hopes for greater understanding among all the peoples of the world are resurrected each Christmas. But while this may be an idea that is dear to you, it can seem like a complex and difficult concept to communicate to your children—expecially if all of your friends have more or less the same background and your winter travels are limited to trips to the grocery store.

But there are some practical ways to help your children become more aware of the other inhabitants of the world. To increase their understanding of the physical size of the planet, you might give them the present of a globe, a poster of the earth as seen from outer space, or an atlas. For example, *The Big Blue Marble Children's Atlas* (Milwaukee: Ideals Publishing Corporation, 1980) is especially designed for children twelve and under.

To help them understand other cultures, you might take advantage of the wonderful gifts available from UNICEF, the United Nations International Children's Emergency Fund. Each year the UNICEF winter catalog features books, games, puzzles, and paper dolls that can help acquaint young children with their counterparts around the globe. The gifts are not only handsome and well made, but your check will go to help children in developing nations the world over. For information on alternative gift sources such as UNICEF and how to contact them, see page 214.

While the dynamics of international affairs are beyond the comprehension of most children, there are a few resources that can help you talk with your children about cooperation versus conflict on a level they can understand. *A Manual of Nonviolence and Children,* from the Friends Peace Committee, helps build nonviolent, cooperative skills in children. It is available by mail order for $4.50 through the Alternatives Resource Center and Bookstore, 1124 Main Street, P.O. Box 1707, Forest Park, GA 30050.

And since peace begins at home, you might want to order your Christmas games from Family Pastimes, a Canadian business that designs games of cooperation rather than competition. Here's a comment from one of their customers: "It's strange to play a game, enjoy the evening, and have no family tensions." To order the catalog, write to: Family Pastimes, R.R. 4, Perth, Ontario, Canada K7H 3C6; or phone 613-267-4819.

Finally, here's a recipe for *kutia,* a Ukrainian Christmas dessert, which has been adapted for children. (*Kutia* is also nice as a breakfast treat.) Let your children have a taste of Christmas from another country.

KUTIA

1 cup wheat berries (whole wheat kernels, available from a health food store)
1 quart water
½ cup boiling water
¼ cup honey (or sugar)
¼ cup poppy seeds
white raisins
chopped nuts
fruit

Boil the berries for 1 hour in water, then drain off starch. Add the boiling water, honey, and poppy seeds. Top with raisins, chopped nuts, and fruit if desired.

This recipe is adapted from *Come and Get It: A Natural Foods Cookbook for Children* by Kathleen M. Baxter (Ann Arbor, Mich.: Children First Press, 1978).

Question 11: *What are some simple traditions that will keep my children from having to wait so long for Christmas to come and then feeling so disappointed when it's over?*

Answer: Here are some suggestions from other parents on how to spread out the joy of the holiday season:

> Last year I made a family calendar for the month of December and drew pictures on it showing when things were going to happen. I drew a tree on the day we were going to get the tree, airplanes on the days that Grandma and Grandpa were flying in and leaving, and a big birthday cake on December 29, which is my five-year-old's birthday. Both of my children looked at it a lot and seemed to get a lot of satisfaction out of knowing when things were going to take place.
>
> I always buy a jigsaw puzzle for the family to put together the day after Christmas. It keeps us all together doing something, but also gives us a quiet way to wind down.
>
> We put a silver cup filled with red-hots on the Christmas tree, and these aren't to be eaten until we take down the tree. It's such a simple thing, but Megan really looks forward to it.
>
> We celebrate each of the twelve days of Christmas with simple activities geared for our children. One day is "Kids-Choose-the-Menu Day," another is "Grandmother Day," and one is "Hear-a-Story-As-Many-Times-As-You-Want Day." On the

twelfth day of Christmas, we have an "End of Christmas Ceremony" and carefully pack away all the decorations. This puts an ending on the season and promises that it will come again.

Question 12: *What should I tell my children about Santa Claus?*

Answer: We hear this particular question over and over again. Parents want to give their children a full measure of holiday joy—including the wonderment of a fat, jolly elf squeezing down a too small chimney. But many parents are concerned about being caught lying to their kids, and others have serious doubts about the modern-day Santa's function—isn't he in reality the patron saint of department stores?

Child psychiatrists, parents, and even children themselves seem to be in a quandary over this one. One three-year-old boy told his mother to put up a SANTA GO AWAY sign on the front door on Christmas Eve. His mother explained that he didn't like the idea of a strange man tramping around *his* house in the middle of the night—not even if he was bearing gifts.

Of all the answers to the Santa Claus dilemma, the one that we like best of all comes from the yellowed, cracking pages of a December 1896 *Good Housekeeping* magazine.

> The problem, then, is before us: What shall we do with Santa Claus? The anxious mother questions, "Would you have me tell my children nothing about Santa Claus? Would you leave all that beautiful part out of our child's life?" By no manner of means.
>
> Tell the child the dear old stories of the good Saint as often as you please, but tell them invariably as myths, as fairy tales. Tell them from babyhood, when the letter will be all he will understand, until he reaches the age when he can grasp the spiritual idea and slough the letter off. If the child is always

told the myth of Santa Claus as a fairy tale, he will have all the childish joy and will have nothing to unlearn. You need not fear that he will lose the child's right to happiness in the story because of this way of presenting it. To a child of three, the spiritual is unintelligible and the tale will be a simple actuality; when he reaches the age of five or six, his mind will readjust it to an ideality.

Tell the child the truth, by all means, but remember that for him, as for all children, some of the deepest truths lie in the realm of fairy tale.

☆

CHAPTER 4:

The Homecoming

In the middle of one of our workshops, a man began enumerating all the things that had bothered him about his family at their last Christmas reunion: his brother had been overly critical of his wife, his father had watched television during most of the family conversations, his mother's cheerfulness had verged on hysteria, and his sister's children had been out of control. He summed up his reaction to the holiday by saying, "I wouldn't mind spending Christmas with my family—if only they'd behave."

His last remark echoes the secret thoughts of a lot of people. While they look forward to seeing their families at Christmas, the reunion is never quite as good as they had hoped. All too often, there's something or someone that disappoints them. Instead of relaxing into a warm family celebration, they find themselves feeling judgmental or aloof, or nursing hurt feelings. And when Christmas is over, they realize that they've missed an important opportunity: there they were surrounded by all the people they really care about, but feelings of deep contentment just weren't there.

So far in this book, we've looked at Christmas from the point of view of each member of the family: the wife, husband, and child. In this chapter we'll explore what happens when they all get together at the Christmas reunion. We've learned that when people have a better understanding of the inner workings of the family Christmas, they go to the reunion with more realistic expectations. And this helps them come closer to realizing the full promise of the celebration.

To begin with, let's take a look at a minor, but not insignificant, part of family gatherings, the physical logistics. As everyone knows, there's a lot of sheer work involved in assembling a large family in one place. The hostess has to spend days cleaning and decorating the house, changing beds, planning meals, stocking the pantry, and coordinating schedules. Meanwhile, the guests have to assemble all their gifts, take care of the animals, make financial and travel arrangements, pack all their suitcases, and secure their houses. These details always take more time and effort than people allow for, and as a family finally piles into a car the day before Christmas to travel down the interstate, it's not uncommon for tempers to be a little frayed.

Then, when everyone's finally gathered together, there are always some minor inconveniences. There's not enough hot water for all the showers, there's always a line at the bathroom, noisy children interrupt Grandpa's nap, teen-agers stay up too late listening to rock music, intrepid joggers wake everyone up in the morning, and there's a constant cleanup in the kitchen.

When everything's going well—when people are getting along, everybody's healthy, and everyone's willing to compromise—these things hardly matter. In fact, they can add to the spirit of fun. There's a feeling of vitality in a house that's teeming with newborns, teen-agers, middle-aged people, and grandparents. However, it helps for people to be mentally prepared for the realities of such a gathering, so that they can take the inevitable ups and downs in stride.

But there's more to the dynamics of a typical Christmas celebration than cold showers, loud rock music, and noisy children. Obviously, a more significant factor in everyone's enjoyment of Christmas is how individual family members relate to each other.

To some degree, this is determined by how well they interact the rest of the year. But, more than people realize, the specific expectations they bring to Christmas play a large role in how they feel about each other at the family reunion.

The main expectation people have at Christmas is that the celebration will bring them closer together. Whether they've been apart for years or see each other every day, they want Christmas to intensify the love that's between them. Their families are the very reason most people "do" Christmas, and their heartfelt wish is that all their family relationships be serene and untroubled.

But for many people, this universal desire for a good family Christmas can turn into unrealistic expectations. Once, just this Christmas, they want everything to be *perfect.* They want to go home to relatives magically transformed into the people they've always wanted them to be. They want past difficulties to be instantly resolved. And they want the whole experience to equal their happiest daydreams.

These are understandable longings. Everyone has a secret wish to be part of a perfect family. But no one ever is. Whenever a door is opened on a family reunion, there will always be imperfect people, complicated relationships, or unfortunate circumstances. Even in the most loving and supportive families, there is always an undercurrent of mixed emotions; a casual remark or a habitual gesture is all it takes to bring back a flood of memories. This is only natural. People who have a long and intimate history together invariably have complex reactions to each other. Freud could have filled a notebook sitting on a couch at a single Christmas reunion. Unless people are emotionally prepared for a houseful of relatives with their real-life strengths and weaknesses, they're going to be disappointed.

This was true for a thirty-two-year-old woman named Sarah, a loan officer in a large bank in an East Coast city. She and her husband decided not to have children, preferring to put their time and energy into their separate careers. Sarah told us about how disappointed she was in her parents the Christmas they came to stay with her. For weeks she had been looking forward to their visit. She and her parents hadn't seen each other in two years, and as she drove to the airport to pick them up, all she could think about was how great it would be to see them. She was especially eager to show them her house. She and her husband had been working on it for months, and had remodeled the spare bedroom just in time for their visit.

When she picked out their familiar faces from the crowd, she ran up to them and gave them each a big hug. But shortly thereafter, she was awash with complex emotions. Her first unexpected reaction came when her father discovered that his new luggage had been slightly scratched on board the plane. All at once she remembered how upset he often got over trivial matters, and she felt her stomach start to tighten. Although her father's anger subsided in a few moments, Sarah still felt on edge. How could she have forgotten about his bad temper? And her anxiety was compounded by the fact that her mother kept going on and on about their new Hartmann luggage and how much it cost. Sarah had also forgotten how status conscious her mother was. For the first time she found herself worrying about how her mother was going to view their slightly run-down neighborhood. It was not a part of town that her parents would ever live in.

On the way home in the car, Sarah felt these confusing feelings subside somewhat as she and her parents caught up on each other's activities. They really were quite loving and charming people, despite their faults. But throughout the rest of their visit, she continued to be disappointed by them. They weren't as perfect as she wanted them to be. For one thing, there was more tension between her mother and father than she remembered. And some of their attitudes seemed narrow and unforgiving. She kept sitting in judgment of them. When the visit was over, she was glad that they had come, but she was equally relieved that they had left.

Like many people, Sarah had set her heart on her relatives' being larger than life, and it was only when she was face to face with them that she saw them as they really were. Then she had to confront her disappointments all over again. Instead of loving and accepting them as imperfect human beings, she found herself being overly critical. If she had made more of an effort to think about the things that had disappointed her about her parents in the past and accepted the fact that they had probably not changed, she could have marshaled her feelings of acceptance and felt less emotionally distant from them.

People from nontraditional families may need to make an even greater effort to accept their families as they really are. Everywhere they look, the two-parent, two-child family is glorified. Christmas commercials show both Mom and Dad trimming the tree while two pajama-clad kiddies help out. Magazine ads show Dad assembling a bicycle on Christmas Eve with Mom smiling in the background. Soft-drink commercials show a family piling into the car to go to Grandma's, with no stops along the way to drop assorted children off at their "real" mom's or dad's. It's always one big, happy, "demographically correct" family settling into a traditional celebration.

This ever present image of the "perfect" family serves only to remind people in nontraditional families of what they don't have. The rest of the year they are given sympathetic support and specific advice on how to create a new, strong family identity. But at Christmas, the rug is pulled out from under them, and they are left alone to cope with their "imperfect" families.

Barbara, the single mother of two girls aged nine and eleven, told us that the first Christmas after her divorce was painfully hard. "I looked around me," she said, "and all I could see were happy couples. And my girls kept grieving for their father. They kept thinking, 'Poor Dad. All alone.' " Everything reminded Barbara and her children of what they had lost.

One of the things that often helps people like Barbara come to terms with their family circumstances is to realize that traditional families—with a homemaker mother, an employed father, and a couple of children—are in the minority. More than 50 percent of all women are employed outside the home. Over 22 percent of all children live with one parent.

When nontraditional families accept the fact that they, like millions of others, are not going to fit into a stereotyped mold, they can start building celebrations that work for them. The second Christmas after her divorce, Barbara was able to do this. She took another look around her and saw that she had more single friends than she thought. So she decided to invite all of the single women she knew and their children to a three-day celebration. "It wasn't really a party," she said. "It was 'Come, be part of my family.' " She carried on her usual traditions with whoever was there. People felt free to sack out on the couch and raid the refrigerator, and the children had a three-day slumber party. She told us that everyone had a wonderful time. "We laughed until our sides ached," she said. "We were women survivors together."

We've met many families like Barbara's that have found ways to create rewarding Christmas celebrations. And whether they were rich or poor, large or small, whether they included two parents or one, they accepted their families for what they were and built on the solid foundation of their real strengths. In the following pages, you will find a few simple exercises that will help you gain new appreciation of your own family, and answers to the most common questions people have about their families at Christmas. The questions and answers concentrate on specific problems, such as how to cope as a single parent, how to handle excessive drinkers, how to ease the strain of a large family reunion, what to do if you are facing Christmas all alone, and how to enrich a small family gathering.

EXERCISES

Exercise 1: THE PERFECT-FAMILY SYNDROME

No family is perfect, but if you can accept your family as it really is, you're going to have a more enjoyable celebration. This first exercise helps you take a look at your family members and explore your hidden expectations for them.

1. In the space below, write down the names of family members that you have complicated or mixed feelings about. Leave a blank space after each name.

2. After each name, write down something that troubles or disappoints you about that person.

Here's an example. Mary did this exercise and made the following comments about her family members:

Person	*What I don't like*
Dad	Drinks too much
Mom	Too uptight and busy
Louise	Overly talkative
Mark	Too withdrawn

3. If you have little reason to believe that people are going to change the characteristics that bother you, look again at each person's name and tell yourself, "I accept the fact that this person will probably . . ." filling in the way that person will most likely behave.

Mary did this part of the exercise and told herself that she would try to accept the fact that her father often drank too much at Christmas. She realized that her mother chose to be so busy and that, even though any number of people offered to help her, she was running the show. Her sister Louise had always talked too much and always would. And her brother Mark often backed away from the family, probably for the very reasons that she did. While she experienced some disappointment in realizing these things about her family, she felt clearheaded about what the visit would be like.

4. Now think of one thing that you especially like about each of the people on your list. Write those desirable qualities down by their names.

Exercise 2: FAMILY STRENGTHS

When people are able to focus on their family strengths and not dwell on their weaknesses throughout the holiday season, they find that Christmas is many times more enjoyable. Whether you have specific family problems or not, this exercise will make you more aware of your family's strong points.

Read the following statements. When a statement is a great family strength, mark it with a star. If it is a lesser strength, mark it with a check. Leave it blank if it does not describe your family at all.

☆ We have common spiritual beliefs or accept each other's different beliefs.
☆ We know how to have fun together.
☆ For the most part, we communicate with each other well.
☆ We openly express our love and affection.
☆ We have similar life-styles and values or accept each other's differences.
☆ We do not have serious money problems.
☆ We usually feel relaxed and comfortable around each other.
☆ We have common Christmas traditions or make a special effort to respect our differences.

☆ We have compatible styles of child-rearing.
☆ We don't have serious alcohol problems.
☆ Other

(If you have few positive responses, make a special effort to fill in the "other" category.)

Questions and Answers

Question 1: *I'm recently divorced. How can my children and I have a good Christmas?*

Answer: Single parents have a lot to contend with at Christmas. Their own feelings of failure and loss are intensified by a celebration that stirs up powerful memories and glorifies the advantages of the traditional family. They must wrestle with these private doubts and sorrows at the same time as they are reassuring their children (who are also coping with the loss of a parent) that all the joy and excitement of Christmas will be theirs. And they must do all of the work involved in providing a good family Christmas by themselves. It's no wonder that many single parents ask whether a good Christmas is possible.

Without denying how difficult Christmas as a single parent can be, we assure you that a good Christmas is within your reach. We've met many single-parent families that find Christmas one of the best times of the year. It may help you to keep in mind that 15 percent of all American families are headed by single parents. It is our *stereotyped image* of the family at Christmas that is out of sync, not the single-parent family itself. It may also help you to remember that married people are not exempt from problems at Christmas, either.

But beyond these realizations, here are some additional suggestions for creating a sense of wholeness at Christmas. First, accept the fact that yours is not a traditional family at Christmas. This acceptance is the necessary first step. The desire to get together again with your ex-spouse can be overwhelming, but the single parents and family counselors we've talked to say it's usually a mistake. Pretending you're a united family again is usually depressing for the adults and confusing for children (although they may ardently desire it), and it delays your progress in finding a new family identity. You need to believe (and demonstrate) that your new family is capable of growing and loving and having fun at Christmas just the way it is.

Second, encourage your children to spend enjoyable time with both parents during the holidays, if possible. Your attitude here is crucial. If either you or your spouse acts left out and full of self-pity, the children may feel guilty. But if you cooperate in making the arrangements and encourage your children to participate enthusiastically in the holiday activities of both parties, Christmas can be a joyful time for them. Some of the children we've talked to even consider themselves lucky because they have two celebrations.

Most single parents tell us how important it is to get these arrangements with ex-spouses made in advance. If visiting arrangements can become traditions, the children gain a sense of security, you are relieved of debilitating negotiations with your ex-spouse, and a definite yearly rhythm is established for the holidays.

Third, plan your own Christmas activities ahead of time. Don't drift through the holidays waiting for something wonderful to happen to you, and don't overload your schedule with Christmas obligations that crowd out the activities you value. Ask yourself what you really need this Christmas to balance the rest of your life. If you need to get away, then consider how you might finance a trip. If you need more social interaction, send out invitations to a party. If you need a more realistic perspective on your own problems, arrange to get involved with those less fortunate.

If you need time with your own children, decline other invitations—even if it means breaking with old traditions.

But one note of caution: don't expect all your planning to make Christmas perfect. Even the most carefully thought-out celebration is subject to the same ebb and flow as everyday living. One woman told us, "I'm trying to broaden my understanding of what a celebration is. Rather than trying to keep all the holes corked and the windows shut and arranging for the hermetic encirclement of the house, I'm trying to allow all of us more freedom."

Fourth, initiate new traditions. One of the most striking things about Christmas is its power to pull you into the past. Something as innocuous as a certain kind of wrapping paper can trigger memories that flood you with feelings you thought you had forgotten. For most people, these memories are pleasant; but for a newly divorced person, they can be a burden. For example, one minister came up to us during a break in a workshop and admitted that talking about Christmas was painful for him. "My wife left me ten months ago and took the kids. Every time you use the words 'family' and 'Christmas' together, I feel like crying. It's all the memories."

Most single parents find that their battle with the Ghost of Christmas Past is easier when they are protected by a shield of new traditions. Old memories don't sting as much when everyone is involved in new activities that signal a new beginning for the family.

Take a look at your Christmas traditions with fresh eyes. Do you really enjoy all the rituals that have become second nature to you at Christmas, or have they become habits? Do they carry meaning for you? Do they suit your new circumstances? One single mother answered no when she asked herself about the traditional Christmas Eve dinner she used to prepare for eight people. It just didn't make sense for her new family of three. So she and her two daughters have begun a new tradition—takeout pizza on Christmas Eve.

Fifth, beware of overdoing the presents to your children. It's natural for many single parents to feel some guilt about their children during and after a divorce. And it's a temptation to try to compensate with Christmas presents. But our conversations with child psychiatrists, single parents, and children themselves show that what children really need from Christmas in times of family stress is the reassurance that they are loved, and the security of knowing that they can grow and learn and be happy in their family just like any other family.

With time, most single parents discover for themselves that overloading their children with presents isn't necessary or even desirable. As one man told us, "I used to feel guilty about being a single father at Christmas. I knew I couldn't provide what a mother could, so I spent a zillion dollars on Christmas presents. Now I know I didn't have to do that. Jesse was getting enough just by my loving him."

Question 2: *Our Christmas is practically spoiled every year by an alcoholic family member. What should we do?*

Answer: This is a very common problem. One out of every ten people in this country has a drinking problem. Chances are, when your family gathers at Christmas, one or more of them are struggling with alcoholism. At one workshop we gave for the parents of grade-school children, we asked the participants to think of a significant Christmas memory. Six out of the ten described unhappy experiences involving alcoholic parents.

When you stop to consider what happens at Christmas, this excessive drinking isn't surprising. Many of the pressures that people regulate successfully the rest of the year are intensified by the wish for a perfect Christmas, and drinking is an escape. Family members who may be uncomfortable or bored with each other take a shortcut to conviviality. Overworked parents look for a fast way to relax before the next round of holiday obligations. And the person alone finds he likes his own company better with each succeeding glass.

On top of this, everything about the secular holiday invites people to indulge themselves. Christmas has always been a festival of abundance, and drinking is one of its principal rituals. But the line between abundance and overabundance is a fine one. All you have to do is scan the December magazines to understand how subtle and all-pervasive this invitation to drink is. The message is clear: people who drink at Christmas are handsome, sexy, affluent, young, intelligent, and classy.

And then there is the Christmas office party. One man described the tradition this way: "Every year my business would host this enormous office party with an open bar on Christmas Eve. My wife would knock herself out doing something nice at home and the kids would be there waiting for me. Many times, I either didn't get home until late, or I came home drunk. The kids would have to be shushed away and apologized to, and the whole thing would be spoiled."

There is no denying that drinking is a problem for countless families at Christmas, but in order to understand this problem better, it's important to realize that not everyone who overdrinks at Christmas is an alcoholic. An alcoholic drinks excessively all year round, whether it is Christmas or not. A "simple excessive drinker" overdoes it on occasions like Christmas.

True alcoholism is a complex problem that succumbs to treatment only when the alcoholic himself decides to seek it. Whatever cajoling or manipulating you do will most likely have no effect. However, one alcoholism counselor we talked with suggested not inviting persons with a history of overdoing it to your Christmas festivities, and telling them plainly why. As he says, "Alcoholics are not fragile people."

If a member of your group is a newly recovered alcoholic (someone who's been sober for one year or less), he or she is vulnerable to the temptations of Christmas drinking. You can do yourself and that person a favor by either serving no alcoholic beverages, or making sure that nonalcoholic alternatives are available. In either case, it's important to treat a recovered alcoholic like a normal person by not making an issue of alcohol one way or the other. And, of course, *never* say to an alcoholic, "Come on, one drink won't hurt you." Although alcoholics know they cannot take even one drink without serious consequences, social pressure is something they don't need.

If you are confronting simple excessive drinkers at Christmas, you have more leverage. Again, straight honest talk about what you expect can be effective. But in addition, planning functions where alcohol is either absent or kept to a ritual minimum can help, even if that means that some people prefer not to accept your invitations.

Excessive drinkers usually like company and will often pressure the people around them to join in. Don't be afraid to say no even if doing so offends them. Because drinking is so often a symptom of boredom and a replacement for genuine involvement with other people, you can also plan activities that get everyone physically active and involved in some way (see the Christmas Revival chapter for suggestions).

If you find *yourself* tempted to drink more than you know you should during the holidays, it might help to remember that alcohol is a depressant. If you are feeling a little down anyway, drinking is liable to make you feel worse. Physical activity and exercise, however, have the opposite effect. Cultivate some activity you enjoy that gets you up and moving about, and you will find that your alcohol intake slows down.

Question 3: *I come from a large family. We have so many family obligations that by the time Christmas is over, we're all exhausted. Is there a way to make our Christmas less hectic?*

Answer: What can you do if your extended-family Christmas feels more like an Olympic marathon than the restful, revitalizing celebration you dream about? Although the answer will be different for every family, we have three suggestions that will help you get closer to your own solutions.

First, ask yourself why you feel exhausted and wrung out during Christmas. Are you trying to see too many people in too short a time? Is traveling the problem? Does your visiting schedule ignore the needs of young children? Or, while your schedule is reasonable, are your relationships with people characterized by conflict and tension? Or does a busy, crowded holiday simply run counter to your idea of what Christmas should be? Once you have identified the source of your uncomfortable feelings, you can start doing something about them.

Second, look for practical solutions, even if this means breaking with tradition. When people have a chance to pinpoint the pressures in their family celebrations, they usually see very quickly what they would like to do differently. Often they realize that what were once enjoyable traditions have become habits that no longer fit their changed circumstances.

One couple with four school-age children decided to make it a rule not to travel anywhere on Christmas Day. They stayed home, resolving to schedule family visits for other times. A couple with junior high schoolers had felt for a long time that they wanted to have Christmas in their own home before their children grew up and moved away. So they decided to invite the grandparents to visit *them* for a change on Christmas next year. And a woman who always felt exhausted at Christmas came to a better understanding of the stresses and strains of a yearly celebration involving her six brothers and sisters and their families. She decided to bow out of the next one and invite her favorite sister and her family for a New Year's visit instead.

Third, communicate your desires to your family. Even the thought of telling Grandma they won't be coming for Christmas gives some people the shivers. Although it isn't possible to make rules about how to approach all family members with changes in Christmas plans, here are some principles to keep in mind. Talk to people well ahead of time. Depending on the situation, you might want to broach the subject to several family members at once during a summer family reunion or at Thanksgiving, or you might decide that a private conversation, letter, or phone call well before Christmas is best. Also, be patient and don't expect to accomplish all the changes you hope for immediately. It can take some people a while to get used to the idea that Christmas isn't going to be the same forever. A seed planted this year could bear fruit next year. Most important of all, take the time to explain your feelings thoroughly and calmly, without blaming others or becoming defensive.

Many of the people in our workshops who have tried this direct, sensitive approach have had success. They say things like "It took my father a while to get used to the idea, but now he accepts it," or "As soon as my brother understood our reasons, he admitted that he was feeling the same way."

And frequently, such proposals are greeted with real enthusiasm and relief. It often happens that several people in a family are feeling the same need for change, and are only waiting for one brave soul to take a stand. A woman told us that a letter she had circulated to her five brothers and sisters suggesting a simpler Christmas opened dialogue with them on a deeper level than ever before.

Question 4: *I live alone and I'm worried about this Christmas. I won't be with my family and I haven't made any other plans.*

Answer: More and more people in this country are living alone. The United States Census Bureau estimates that there were over seventeen million people living alone in this country in 1979. Many of them go home to extended families for Christmas, but an increasing number have no close family or, for a variety of reasons, decide not to rejoin their relatives during the holidays. Over the last few years, we have talked with a handful of single people who have chosen to spend Christmas alone. There are a number of things you can do alone that you cannot do as part of a family gathering. If spiritual experiences are important to you at Christmas, you can decide to spend time in prayer, meditation, or reading. You can spend time outdoors hiking, skiing, camping. You can play your favorite music for hours on end. You can eat when and what you want and generally set your own schedule.

One man, a hairdresser, told us that his job required so much day-to-day contact and conversation that he relished the idea of Christmas Eve and Christmas Day alone. When we asked him whether he did anything special, he told us that he saved up special reading material for these two days, prepared his favorite meal of fried shrimp for Christmas dinner, and put his favorite madrigal music on the stereo. Another woman we talked with made it a tradition to reserve her aunt's beach cabin for the few days surrounding Christmas. Because she was an artist and found the solitude of the ocean restful and refreshing, she viewed these few days as a great privilege. Her only nods to Christmas were a big fire in the fireplace, homemade eggnog, and the reading of Dylan Thomas's *A Child's Christmas in Wales* on Christmas Eve. But, as she hastened to tell us, when she got back to town, she also made it a tradition to balance her solitude by throwing a huge New Year's Eve party for everyone she knew.

Although there are some people who look forward to Christmas alone, the overwhelming majority like to celebrate with other people. If you want your celebration to be social, you will probably find that you have a lot of options. To some degree, whether you perceive your lack of family as an irretrievable loss or as a chance to explore new options depends on your attitude. Here are some suggestions to help you see the possibilities.

First, redefine your idea of "family." Most people think of family as a group of people fixed for them by the accidents of blood and marriage. Whether they like their brothers and sisters and aunts and uncles or not, there they are. But more and more people these days are picking and choosing the people they wish to spend Christmas with. They are rearranging themselves into groups held together by mutual goals and affection that function in the same relaxed, supportive ways as traditional families. You may know several unattached, compatible people who would welcome an opportunity to gather at your house and spend Christmas with you. This kind of "family-by-choice" gathering is common and accepted at Christmas these days.

Second, get involved in helping others. A lot of people are frustrated because they do not have the time or the flexibility at Christmas to do the charitable things that they would like. You have just such an opportunity. Several of the single people we have talked to have committed themselves to food drives, hospital and nursing home visits, or other selfless activities at Christmas and gotten immense pleasure from them. They found that it made them feel good to help other people, and that they helped themselves by gaining a broader perspective on their problems.

Third, allow yourself to respond to your own impulses. There is a wonderful freedom in being able to act on the spur of the moment. One man with no family told us that just before Christmas the previous year, he had split up with his girlfriend and moved to a new town. He found himself alone for the holidays. At first he was fearful, but he decided to trust himself and his resilience. On Christmas morning, he got the idea of making some banana bread and taking it around to his neighbors, whom he had not had a chance to meet. He told us that their reception of a strange man bearing slightly soggy, warm banana bread on Christmas Day was heartwarming. Even if they were in the middle of their own family activities, they stopped, asked him in for a drink, and got acquainted.

Fourth, accept invitations from families at Christmas. It's the rare family that hasn't, at one time or another, taken in an unattached person for Christmas. Far from being an intrusion, the new person becomes a positive factor in the celebration. These families not only enjoy the introduction of "new blood" into their gatherings, but also feel good about dispelling someone else's loneliness. When we ask people to tell us about their childhood Christmases, they often call up fond memories of a single person who spent Christmas with the family.

There is no reason single people can't have full, happy Christmases. If you know yourself well enough to know what you need, approach the holiday with a spirit of adventure and confidence, and do some advance planning, you will find that Christmas is a time you look forward to.

Question 5: Our family is so small that I always feel something is missing at Christmas. What can we do to have a better celebration?

Answer: We are conditioned to think of a thirty-pound turkey roasting in the oven and fourteen dinner plates set around the extended dining-room table at Christmas. On some deep level, most of us want to be surrounded during our celebrations by a sea of smiling, familiar faces, made dear by the bonds of love and marriage. When we think of Christmas, we think of big families; it's a hard habit to break.

And we maintain this dream even though today's families are getting smaller. In 1980, the average number of persons per household in the United States was 3.31. The average number of children was 1.07. It's true that these small units can combine into larger family groups at Christmas and live out the American Christmas dream, but there are an increasing number of small families that spend Christmas by themselves. Either they don't have the money to travel, the distance is too great, or they are emotionally cut off from their larger families. Then they are left with the reality of a missing spouse, or too few grandparents, or not enough children or cousins or aunts and uncles at Christmas.

While some people adapt to a small Christmas just fine, others have trouble getting over the nagging feeling that something is wrong. If you find yourself feeling that your family isn't large enough, here are some suggestions.

Make an effort to appreciate all the advantages of a small family. Because there are so few of you, you avoid many of the problems that surface in large family gatherings. You don't have to take into account the preferences, moods, and habits of a large group of independent adults and their unpredictable offspring. You probably don't have to spend as much money or go to as much trouble to prepare for the holiday. And you have a greater chance of finding the peace and quiet that is so important for a deep enjoyment of the holiday.

When you take advantage of these pluses, new opportunities open up for you. One single woman told us about a refreshing change in her style of celebration. "It used to be just my mother, my father, and me sitting down to a big Christmas dinner and opening presents all by ourselves," she said. "Although we liked each other's company, there was this emptiness, and I kept wondering what else we could do. My father had the inspiration. He suggested that we go to a good restaurant for Christmas dinner instead, and spend a few days going to the best museums and galleries in Chicago. We had a wonderful time together."

You may also wish to include non–family members in your celebration. If you still feel that more is better, you can enlarge your definition of "family" by reaching out to nonrelatives and drawing them into your celebration. There are always people around who would appreciate an invitation to your Christmas dinner. There are charities to assist, nursing homes to visit, widowed friends to console, young people to mother, and other small families like yours that would appreciate more people around on Christmas Day.

☆

CHAPTER 5:

Inside the Christmas Machine

Over the years, our workshop has been sponsored by a wide variety of organizations, including community colleges, churches of seven major denominations, parents' groups, ministerial associations, and social service agencies. But once, just once, it was offered as a "holiday event" in a large department store.

The irony did not escape us. There we were, offering our "Unplug the Christmas Machine" workshop in the throbbing heart of the Christmas Machine itself. Our workshop was held in a conference room on the tenth floor of the department store, the same floor as all the holiday gift wrap, Christmas cards, and decorations. And in order to get to the workshop, everyone had to file past the "Designer Christmas Collection," an elegant display of old-fashioned rocking horses, Colonial Christmas tree ornaments, and eighty-dollar antique dolls. Stationed right outside our door was a twelve-foot-high Christmas tree made out of stuffed, green satin triangles.

In good faith, we made some concessions to the department store. We changed the title of our workshop from "Unplug the Christmas Machine" to the more benign "How to Have the Christmas You Really Want," and made a pact between us to focus our comments on how Christmas affects family life, rather than holiday commercialism. But we also made it clear to the coordinator of the event that when people are given the chance to examine their family celebrations in detail, they often decide to scale down their gift-giving.

As it turned out, the people who came to this particular workshop were more upset than most about Christmas commercialism. The very first woman to speak said that she didn't enjoy buying gifts for four of the people on her gift list. They were all wealthy, and she could never figure out what to buy them. "No matter what I come up with," she said, "they can always go out and buy the next brand up the ladder. Christmas seems like an overabundance of things nobody wants or needs." The next person picked up her train of thought. "The only thing that seems to matter at Christmas is how much money you spend," he said. "It's pure economics. And when the spirituality leaves the holiday in favor of materialism, it leaves a very large hole."

Later in the day, when we asked everyone in the group to create a fantasy of an ideal Christmas celebration, not one of the more than forty people in the workshop described a Christmas with elaborate gifts. In fact, if gifts were mentioned at all, they were simple handmade presents or intangible gifts like love and acceptance.

Even as these people were sharing their visions of an ideal Christmas, a noisy crowd of shoppers just outside the room made it difficult to hear, so a man in the back of the room got up and closed the door. As he sat back down he said, "Here we are talking about cutting back on gifts in the city's largest department store at the height of the shopping season. I bet this is exactly what it felt like to be inside the Trojan horse."

No matter where we have given our workshop, what we have called it, or how little encouragement we have given people to talk about gift problems, there have always been a large number of people with mixed feelings about Christmas presents. Often, their positive and negative feelings run neck and neck. On the positive side, they like the fact that Christmas encourages them to reach out to family and friends. They get genuine pleasure out of giving presents to the special people in their lives. And many people like the fact that making or buying gifts exercises their creativity. It can be very satisfying to choose just the right gift for each individual or to lovingly craft presents. And there's yet another reason so many people enjoy holiday gift-giving. When Christmas is over, everyone has presents to use and enjoy that serve as reminders of the people who gave them. The whole year can be made richer by the gifts exchanged at Christmas.

But despite these positive aspects, many people have problems with Christmas gift-giving. While they are just as eager as anyone else to wish their family and friends a merry Christmas, they feel that the whole tradition has gotten out of hand. And when they stop to examine their gift-giving habits, they realize that they have sincere and unselfish reasons for wanting to make changes.

For example, many people have problems with elaborate holiday gift-giving for the simple reason that they can no longer afford it. A grandmother with five children and twelve grandchildren told us that when all her friends and relatives were totaled up, she was buying at least thirty gifts each Christmas. Before her husband had retired, this seasonal outpouring of love and generosity had been manageable. But now that they were living on Social Security, buying that many presents had become a financial burden. With each present she bought, she felt a twinge of anxiety: How were they going to come up with the money to pay for all those gifts?

Other people are unhappy with traditional holiday gift-giving because exchanging typical consumer goods at Christmas has little value to them. It seems pointless to spend weeks struggling to think of novel gift ideas for relatives who have so many things already. These people would rather exchange simple handmade gifts, or spend the time and energy they would normally sink into Christmas presents just being with the people they care about.

Finally, many Christians are unhappy with the fact that the spiritual message of Christ has to compete with the want-me, buy-me message of the merchants. When they stop to think about the simple way Christ lived his life and his concern for "the least of these," celebrating his birth with a multibillion-dollar exchange of video games, popcorn poppers, designer jeans, sports equipment, and expensive adult toys seems strangely inappropriate. As one man said, "It's hard to see Christ in all the electric carving knives and shaving cream."

For these reasons and more, many people want to simplify their holiday gift-giving to bring it more into line with their resources, values, and beliefs. While they want to give people symbols of their love and affection, they aren't convinced that the tradition has to be so expensive and elaborate.

How did Christmas gift-giving get to be so complicated, anyway? In the 1800s, Christmas presents were primarily for children, and when adults did exchange gifts, they were simple presents like fountain pens and handkerchiefs, and were called "holiday notions." But in the early part of this century, all this began to change. At the end of World War I, there were fears that the boom times of the war years were going to be followed by a stagnant economy, so advertisers did their best to stimulate peacetime buying. Holiday presents were a logical target. People were already giving gifts to each other at Christmas—even though they were usually modest items—and the idea of generosity was firmly embedded in the celebration; all the merchants had to do was capitalize on it. Gradually, the Christmas Machine began to build up steam, and ads like the following (from *The New York Times* of December 15, 1919) began to appear in newspapers and magazines: "Don't give your family and friends frivolous gifts that are sure to disappoint, buy them worthy gifts that will let them know how much you care."

Another Christmas ad from the same period features a sketch of a disdainful-looking man smoking a cigarette. The ad copy advises women that their husbands will be highly critical of their holiday offerings unless they come from a certain elegant men's clothing store. A woman who was accustomed to slipping a necktie or some tobacco into Pappa's stocking was being issued a blunt warning that she had better put more money and thought into what she gave him if she wanted a contented husband.

From that point on Christmas started becoming big business. And despite the fact that we are now spending an estimated twenty billion dollars a year on Christmas, the sales pressure continues unabated. From the first "preholiday" sale in October to the last "post-Christmas" sale in mid-January, Americans are deluged with Christmas advertising. However, in recent years a more sophisticated public has required more sophisticated tactics. Today, clever advertisers beguile us with woodwind renditions of sixteenth-century French Christmas carols, invite people into shopping malls that claim to have the "Dickens Christmas spirit" because they are decorated with Victorian Christmas ornaments, and pack away the department store tinsel in favor of more tasteful displays of live poinsettias.

In all fairness, it must be stated that ads are only one of the reasons gift-giving has grown ever more elaborate. In the early years of this century, Americans were eager to share the bounty of an increasingly wealthy nation. People who grew up in the more austere nineteenth century were delighted to give their families the opulent celebrations that they, themselves, had never had. It seemed like a positive step to go from giving their children presents like doughnuts and rag dolls to showering Schwinn bikes and Lionel trains on them.

But most people today grew up with a fairly lavish celebration, and for many of them, the Christmas of the 1980s seems like a festival of *over*abundance. An ever more sumptuous celebration seems out of harmony with their social consciousness, their concern for the environment, or their need to return to more basic human values.

Unfortunately, when people contemplate making a change in their gift-giving habits—even a relatively simple one—they run straight into some social taboos. Although few people are aware of it, an elaborate unspoken code governs the seasonal exchange of gifts. These hidden rules help establish order in a complicated social situation, but they also are a key factor in keeping the tradition expensive and elaborate. What are these rules? Read through the following ten axioms and see if they ring a bell.

The Self-Defeating Gift-Giving Rules

1. Give a gift to everyone you expect to get one from.
2. If someone gives you a gift unexpectedly, you should reciprocate that year, even if you had no previous intention of giving that person a present. (Some people have wrapped gifts set aside for just such an occasion.)
3. When you give someone a gift, you should plan to give that person a gift every year thereafter.
4. The amount of time and money you spend on a gift should be directly proportional to how much you care about the recipient.
5. The gift that you give someone should be equal in monetary value and/or personal significance to the one you receive from that person.
6. The presents you give someone should be fairly consistent over the years.
7. If you give a gift to a person in one category (for example: coworkers or neighbors) you should give gifts to everyone in that category. And these gifts should be similar.
8. The gifts you give your children should be equal in number and monetary value, while at the same time suiting the unique qualities of each child.
9. Men should *not* give gifts to their male friends, unless the gifts are alcoholic beverages. Women, however, are encouraged to give gifts to their female friends, and those gifts should *not* be alcohol.
10. Homemade gifts are more "meaningful" than store-bought ones.

While it is humorous to see these hidden gift-giving conventions written down in black and white, when most people think about it, they remember occasions where they had considerable influence. For example, a good friend of ours named Sharon told us about the following actual gift-exchange, which grew increasingly complicated precisely because of these hidden rules.

Sharon's story started out simply enough. Her original intention was to give all of her friends baked goods for Christmas. But a problem came up when a friend named Meg told Sharon that she had found a "fabulous" gift for her. Sharon knew right away that the loaf of bread she had been planning to give Meg would not match Meg's gift to her (*a potential violation of Rule 5: exchange gifts of equal value*), so she went out and bought Meg a rather expensive present.

Sharon thought that this maneuver had resolved the dilemma, but the situation grew more complex later that week, when Meg called to say that their mutual friend, Anne, wanted to be there when they opened gifts. This new development complicated matters because Sharon had also been planning to give Anne simple baked goods for Christmas. But now that Anne was going to be there, Sharon would have to get an equally nice gift for her, too (*or break Rule 7: give similar gifts to people in the same category*).

The actual gift-opening turned out to be even more emotionally difficult than Sharon had anticipated. Meg's gift to her was worth at least twice as much as the one she had bought for Meg, despite her efforts to even out the exchange (*breaking Rule 5 after all*). And Anne, the innocent bystander, was visibly confused by the unexpectedly high value of all the gifts being exchanged. She gave both Meg and Sharon simple scarves, and was surprised to find herself caught in the middle of such an extravagant gift-exchange (*another violation of Rule 5*).

If the ten gift-giving rules were followed rigorously, there would be no way to simplify gifts, because they lock everyone into a tit-for-tat mentality and assure that each year's offerings will be at least equal to last year's. But when people are determined to make their Christmas presents more a genuine expression of their feelings and less a rule-bound ritual, they can find ways to circumvent the hidden conventions. One way for people to get around them is to openly declare their intentions. Imagine how short and sweet Sharon's story would have been if she had said to Meg at the outset, "It's very generous of you to buy me such an expensive gift, but I only have a simple one for you."

Just being more aware of the gift-giving rules and how they further or frustrate their goals gives many people the courage to do what they really feel is best. For example, a woman named Sara told us that in previous years she and her husband used to go through a convoluted weighing and measuring with each present they gave. First they tried to remember exactly what they had previously given certain people. Then they thought about what those people had given them. Finally, they tried to choose a gift that would be exactly equivalent to the one they thought they were going to receive. But the year after attending our workshop, she and her husband spent some time talking about gifts and decided to be less conscious of the rules. They decided to just pick out things that felt right to give and leave it at that. "We felt as if a weight had been lifted from us," she said.

Some people get around the restrictive gift-giving rules by getting together with family and friends to invent new ones. For example, one family from Oregon agreed to violate Rule 6 (gifts should be consistent from year to year) by giving each other explicit permission to vary their gifts. They decided to do this because they rarely had the same amount of time or energy to spend on gifts from year to year, making it hard to maintain a set standard. "Now if we're short of money or time, we just give what we comfortably can without having to apologize or feel guilty," said one of the family members. "I don't think any one of us could have felt this freedom without our getting together to talk about it."

Other families have agreed to deescalate gift-giving by giving each other token presents, rewriting Rule 4 (gifts must be an exact measure of your regard for the recipient). One such family has started a tradition of buying gifts at garage sales. While secondhand gifts may offend some people, everyone in this particular family loves them. "We're all good scroungers," explained the mother. "And none of us have much money. So we prowl around secondhand stores and garage sales looking for things." Because the members of this family don't build up hopes for expensive, shiny new gifts, they can approach the family gift-exchange with a spirit of fun and humor. "Other people probably think we're strange," said a teen-age daughter. "But we all look forward to opening our gifts and usually end up in hysterical laughter."

To some people, giving gifts of their time and energy seems a more genuine way to show affection than giving the usual store-bought gifts. For example, a fifty-year-old farmwife named Merrily wrote us a letter telling us that her family's gift to her was a "year of Wednesdays." She explained that her husband and daughter had volunteered to do all her household and farm chores each Wednesday, provided she used that time for creative pursuits. For over twenty years, she had been running the household and managing the family farm, filling in her few remaining hours with civic duties. Now, she told us, she was gratefully using this gift of time to take calligraphy lessons, practice the piano, write, and paint.

One couple learned that *not* giving *any* gift to one of their sons turned out to be the best gift of all. Joan told us that for years her son Peter had been telling her not to get him anything special for Christmas because he didn't need material things. But she and her husband had ignored his request because they didn't feel that they had any other way to relate to him at Christmas. Besides, they would have felt funny about giving a gift to one son and not the other. "So we always got Peter something," Joan explained, "and he would be polite about receiving it."

One year, she and her husband spent some time thinking about what their son was really trying to tell them. As a result, they decided to take the money they would have spent on Peter and donate it to a friend of the family who was a kidney dialysis patient. "We told Peter about it the week before Christmas," Joan said, "and he felt really good about it. It gave him a deep sense of pleasure to think that the money was going to help a family friend."

When people choose their gifts with love and sensitivity, not with an eye to the rules, the holiday takes on fresh meaning. What everyone wants from Christmas is an exchange of genuine love and goodwill, not a swap of material goods. Some people find that a traditional gift-exchange gives them the feelings they're looking for, but others feel the need to create new traditions. In the following exercises, you will have a chance to clarify your feelings about your family gift-giving. Then you can read answers to the questions we hear most often about gifts. In the Appendix there are specific gift-giving suggestions. Gifts to children are also discussed in the chapter on children.

Exercises

Exercise 1: GIFT INVENTORY
In the space provided below, list all the people you gave gifts to last year. Be sure to include friends, neighbors, coworkers, and children of friends or neighbors. Put a dollar sign by each person you spent more than ten dollars on.

Exercise 2: FOUR GIFT FANTASIES
1. Imagine yourself in the following situations and check the ones that are most appealing to you.

a. You open the mail one morning and discover that you have inherited $250 to spend on Christmas presents this year.
b. You are given two weeks of absolutely free time to devote to making Christmas gifts.
c. Every member of your family is excited about exchanging simpler and less expensive gifts.
d. Everyone in the nation decides to eliminate gift-giving from the celebration. There is no holiday advertising, no gift-giving obligations. People celebrate Christmas by joining with family and friends, by feasting, and with family and community Christmas activities.

2. Judging by your reactions to these imaginary situations, what changes would you ideally like to make in your family gift-giving?

Exercise 3: GIFT MEMORIES

1. Think back over past Christmases and remember a gift that you received that gave you great pleasure. What did you especially like about that gift?

2. Now remember a gift you received that made you feel anxious, confused, angry, or disappointed. What was it about that situation that bothered you?

3. All in all, what kind of gifts do you feel best about receiving and giving?

Questions and Answers

Question 1: *I'd like to simplify my gift-giving but I'm not sure about the reaction of my family and friends. What should I do?*

Answer: It can seem difficult at first to change entrenched gift-giving habits. You may be exchanging gifts with ten, twenty, or thirty people, and they probably have a wide range of values and feelings about Christmas presents. But if *you* feel that your gift-giving has gotten out of hand, chances are many of the others do, too. Some of the people on your list may actually prefer making a special effort to get together with you during the holiday season in place of exchanging gifts, and others may find it a relief to give fewer or simpler presents. And the only way to find out is by talking with them.

But first, it might help you to get a better idea of which people on your list would be most receptive to simplifying gifts, and then to do some more thinking about alternatives.

Here is an exercise to help you survey your gift list. Look back at Exercise 1 above and place a check mark by the name of any person on the list who you think might welcome an invitation not to exchange gifts. (They might be distant relatives, or casual acquaintances who would find it a relief not to exchange gifts. On the other hand, they might be very good friends or close relatives who would prefer another way of making contact at Christmas.) Put a plus sign by anyone who you think might be willing to talk about exchanging fewer or simpler gifts. Put an X by anyone who you think would be opposed to any change whatsoever.

Now you have a better idea of how many people might be willing to explore gift-giving options. But what kind of changes do you want to suggest? Below, we have listed the five most common gift-giving alternatives. All of them work well for some families. Read through them and check the ones that seem most suitable for yours.

1. **Name drawing.** Put the family names in a hat and draw the name of one person to buy or make a gift for.
2. **Trimming a few names.** Talk with the people who you think might welcome an invitation not to exchange gifts.
3. **Family gifts.** Give one gift per household instead of a gift for each separate individual.
4. **Just for kids.** Keep giving presents to young children only.
5. **Alternative gifts.** Give simple handmade gifts or gifts of

service; or spend your money on a special trip or vacation together.

Keep in mind that you don't have to find one alternative that works for everyone. You can make separate arrangements with each household.

Once you have a better idea of the kind of change you want to propose, you will want to talk with your friends and family as early in the year as possible. Many people like to get their gift-buying out of the way early in the fall. If it's too late *this* year to make new arrangements, get together now to talk about what you want to do next year. (Doing this a year ahead of time is actually an ideal arrangement, because you will be talking about what you like and don't like about gift-giving while the experience is fresh in your mind, and you will have a whole year to adjust to any changes.)

When you talk with your family and friends, keep five points in mind. (1) Choose a relaxed and comfortable time when people are in an accepting mood. (2) Be clear about your reasons for wanting to make changes. (3) Be open to other people's opinions and suggestions. (4) Keep in mind that other people probably have done less thinking about gifts than you have and want some time to consider before they come to any conclusions. (5) Don't be afraid to experiment. You might want to try out an alternative gift-giving arrangement for a year and see how it works, then make some changes the following year.

We have learned that there can be an important side benefit to talking with your family about gift alternatives. Many people have told us that they had made better contact with their friends and relatives by getting together to talk about gifts than they had in years. It gave them a chance to share their good feelings about each other and become better acquainted with each other's values. And whatever their ultimate gift-giving decisions, they found that they were drawn closer together.

Question 2: *I would like to make all my gifts, but I never have enough time. What should I do?*

Answer: Handmade gifts seem like ideal Christmas presents to many people. They are more personal, less expensive, and often more satisfying to both the giver and the receiver. In fact, handmade gifts are so welcome at Christmas that many people feel they *should* make their gifts even when they don't have the time, talent, or internal motivation. Before you try to squeeze hours of gift-making into your busy life, stop and honestly examine your feelings. If you find that you enjoy making gifts and they have high priority for you, turn to the Appendix and look for especially quick and easy homemade gift ideas.

Question 3: *I've felt uncomfortable opening gifts as long as I can remember. Why is that?*

Answer: You have a lot of company. Most adults discover that they get more pleasure out of giving presents than receiving them. One reason you feel anxious opening gifts may be that it makes you feel as if you're on stage. Like most people, you probably feel the need to act pleased no matter what you find in the package, because you don't want to hurt anyone's feelings.

Another reason for your discomfort may be that you have hidden wishes that are not being fulfilled. It's very common for people to secretly wish for special gifts from their spouses or parents that show exactly how much they care. While the dreamers may know that this is unrealistic (the gift-givers may be poor at choosing presents, or have very little time or money to devote to gift-giving), they still harbor the wish.

Finally, you may be reacting to the fact that many gifts carry hidden messages. An example would be a husband's gift of a too small, slinky dress to his overweight wife. Gift-giving is a complex social phenomenon that puts the relationships between individuals into tangible form, and the messages hidden in the gifts are often as complicated as the relationships.

Question 4: My husband and I have very different ideas on gift-giving. How can we come to see eye to eye?

Answer: You and your husband each have a long and complicated history involving Christmas presents and, as with most people, your past experiences with gifts are probably a determining factor in your present attitudes. One woman told us that gifts were not very important to her but her husband went overboard with them each Christmas. She couldn't understand this until he told her about his childhood celebrations. When he was young, he had often felt shortchanged by his family at Christmas. His brother and sisters always seemed to get the better gifts. As an adult, he wanted to make sure other people didn't feel slighted. You may find that if you and your husband shared some of your earlier associations with gifts, you would understand each other better.

On the other hand, your problem may be one of differing values, not different Christmas histories. If this is the case, sit down and share your opinions. Be prepared for some strong emotions. Many people have intense feelings about what role gifts should play in the celebration. You may find it easier to accommodate the other person's point of view once you understand the sincere feelings behind it. Finally, you may need to work out a compromise. For example, you may decide to let each spouse take responsibility for giving gifts to his or her own family members, or work out a balance between your points of view.

☆

CHAPTER 6:

The Gift of Joy

Rose is a tax accountant and the fifty-year-old mother of two teen-age children. She told us that no matter how much energy she puts into Christmas, she often feels disappointed by the celebration. "I don't know if it's regret over what might have been, or memories of what used to be—all I know is that in recent years, Christmas has seemed rather pointless," she said. "When you take away the fuss and the bother, Christmas is just another big meal."

This is a common complaint. Many people tell us that they have a vague feeling of emptiness at Christmas. Even though they are doing things they have looked forward to all year long and are surrounded by their favorite friends and relatives, they still have the feeling that something is missing. For some reason, the vivid reds and greens of the holiday season merge into gray, and they find themselves just going through the motions of rejoicing.

At first, some people have a hard time explaining exactly what's wrong with Christmas because on the surface everything looks fine. But when they take a closer look, many of them realize that their celebrations lack depth and meaning. It's not enough that Christmas be a family birthday party or the biggest social event of the year. They want to be moved by the celebration.

When they decorate, they want the result to be more than a beautiful house. They want to look around them and be filled with an air of expectancy. When they write a check to a charity, they don't want to be mentally computing the tax deduction. They want to be filled with genuine compassion for the people they are helping. And when they attend a worship service, they don't want to be just passive consumers of an hour's religious entertainment. They want to be filled with the spirit of God. At Christmas people want to reach down inside themselves and come up with feelings that are better, bigger, more joyful, more loving, and more lasting than their everyday ones.

But as the following workshop conversation shows, many people go through Christmas without this deep sense of joy.

First woman: You know, something I'm just beginning to realize is how self-centered my Christmas has become. Here I am talking about how my house looks and what other people think of me. I'm not reaching out, not doing things for people who don't have all that I do.

First man: Well, in our family, we do a few charitable things. But most of them are pretty mechanical. Pleas for money come in the mail and I write out checks. But I'm not really involved in any of the causes. I just save myself the guilt.

Second woman: I get to feeling very guilty at this time of year because we are not associated with a church. I think we should be more spiritual at Christmas. Both my husband and I went to Sunday school as kids, but we haven't raised our kids that way. Christmas is a church holiday. I feel my family is missing something.

Third woman: I'm Christian. And I go to the candlelight service on Christmas Eve. That's where Christmas comes alive for me. But on Christmas Day—when there are thirty-five people jammed together eating too much and giving presents that nobody needs—that's not Christmas. There's a big spiritual hole there.

Second man: I know what you mean. We go to church and have Advent ceremonies at home. But Christmas Eve and Christmas Day are totally irreligious. I think this adds to my feeling of emptiness. The spiritual message isn't there when it should be.

As these remarks show, both Christians and non-Christians can feel a spiritual emptiness at Christmas. Although the celebration has a fundamental religious significance for Christians, they must find a way to make these beliefs come alive. In a broad sense, both Christians and non-Christians are asking the same questions: How can Christmas connect me with ideas and experiences larger than myself? How can I share my blessings with other people? How can the celebration make me feel most whole and happy?

When people don't find satisfactory answers to these questions, some take it as a personal failure. What's wrong with *me* that I don't feel loving and generous and closer to God? Why haven't I felt even one moment of pure happiness? When they look around them, they see that others seem to have all the joy that eludes them, and they often feel alone in their disappointment. Then there are people who look outside themselves for the source of their discontent. Many blame Christmas commercialism. To them, the constant emphasis on the buying and selling of holiday happiness robs the celebration of its significance. They wonder if it's even possible to have a value-centered holiday when so many forces conspire against them. Other people attribute their lukewarm feelings to the idea that Christmas is basically a children's holiday and they've gotten too old to enjoy it. They look back nostalgically to their childhood Christmases and try to accept that those moments of joy are all in the past.

But for most people, the real problem with Christmas isn't that they are spiritually bankrupt or that Christmas is devoid of meaning. It's simply that they haven't taken the time to define for themselves what's most important to them about Christmas.

A lot of people go through the holiday season without a clear sense of what they value. While they have planned the details of their celebrations right down to the kind of cranberry sauce to serve at Christmas dinner, they haven't stopped to ask themselves the all-important question: Why am I celebrating Christmas? They rely on habit, other people's priorities, commercial pressures, or random events to determine the quality of their celebrations. But this is rarely successful. People need to make conscious choices, because Christmas offers them so many possibilities. It's a time to celebrate the birth of Christ, the pleasures of family life, the importance of friendship, the delight of creating a beautiful home environment, the need for world peace, the desire to be charitable, and a host of other important values. When people don't sort out which of these ideas are most important to them, the celebration can seem fractured and superficial.

But choosing among all the rich possibilities of Christmas is not always easy. Often, people must choose between activities of seemingly equal value. For example, they must decide whether to spend their limited funds to buy more gifts for family and friends, or to make a contribution to an important charity. They must weigh the value of having a quiet, relaxed celebration against that of entertaining special friends. And if they are Christians, they must ask themselves what's more important, working for the church or spending more time with their families.

When people haven't resolved these larger issues, they find it hard to make the dozens of small decisions that confront them every day of the holiday season. For example, Louise, a young woman in her late twenties, told us about a puzzling experience she had had the year before. In the weeks just before Christmas, her mother had been feeling a little glum, and Louise decided that buying her mother an early Christmas present—something a little extravagant that she wouldn't buy for herself—might cheer her up. Louise deliberated on what to buy her mother for several days, and finally settled on a print that she had seen in an art studio.

One rainy afternoon right before Christmas, Louise left work to buy the print. On the way, she turned on her car radio and heard the announcer make a plea for more toy donations to the local charity drive. He said that the demand for children's gifts was much greater than expected, and that many children would go without toys unless people responded immediately.

Louise pulled the car over to the side of the road and sat there for a few minutes thinking about the announcement. How could she spend fifty dollars on an extra present for her mother when there were children facing Christmas without any toys at all? She decided that she couldn't buy the print after all. So she turned around and drove back home.

But the confusing thing to Louise was that she never donated the money to the toy drive. "I didn't do anything," she said. "I just went home and tried to forget about the print." Louise wanted to do something nice for her mother, but she felt guilty about spending so much extra money on someone who was comfortable already. And she wanted to help the children, but she wasn't clear enough about her priorities to actually go ahead and make the donation.

Like Louise, many people are so overwhelmed by the competing possibilities of the celebration that they find themselves unable to make any choices at all. And they often end up feeling guilty or disappointed by their inactivity. But other people have the opposite reaction. They see value in a wide range of holiday activities, and because they are energetic and resourceful, they try to squeeze them all in. These are the people who lead the community charity drive, make all their own tree ornaments from recycled objects, put on Christmas parties for the neighborhood children, make cookies for nursing homes, sew matching outfits for their nieces and nephews, and direct the church Christmas program. They want to do it all. Unfortunately, their pleasure in all these activities diminishes with each new one that's added. And they end up feeling numb and tired, cut off from the deep satisfaction they hoped all this activity would bring them.

Other people make the wrong choices. They don't do too little or too much; they simply put their time and energy into activities and projects that aren't right for them. For example, most people put a lot of time, money, and energy into gift-giving. But when they sit down and sort out their values, many realize that spending time with their families, giving money to charity, or nurturing their spiritual lives—some other part of the celebration—is more important to them. For years they've been channeling the bulk of their resources into a part of Christmas that has only limited value to them, and still they wonder why the celebration seems so shallow and meaningless.

It's clear that being unsure of their values is the source of many people's unhappiness at Christmas. But we've been encouraged by how quickly and easily people can decide what's most important to them. All they need to do is to become more aware of the need to make choices, have some sense of what those choices are, and set aside a little time to reflect on them. With just a few minutes of prayer, meditation, or conscious decision-making, most people gain a much better sense of how Christmas should be. At the end of this chapter we've included an exercise that will help you take a look at all the values that are competing for your attention at Christmas and rank them in order of priority. This simple exercise may be all you need to gain a better understanding of what's most important to you during the holiday season.

We had a demonstration of how quickly this can happen when we were at a radio station talking with a man who was about to interview us on a talk show. Just before we went on the air, we handed him a copy of the values exercise that's at the back of this chapter. Even though we were scheduled to go on the air in just two minutes, he was intrigued by the exercise and decided to see how much of it he could complete. In that short amount of time, he was able to identify one of his major problems with Christmas: he wasn't spending enough time with his kids. His children's happiness was his top priority, but he had allowed a lot of other things to come first. He resolved to go home and talk with his wife about cutting out some of their social obligations so he could spend more quiet evenings at home with his family.

Like this radio announcer, many people decide to make some adjustments in their holiday plans once they have a clear sense of what's important to them. For example, they may decide to cut back on other activities in order to spend more time with their families, or they may decide to help out with a charity drive so they can translate their generous impulses into action.

This self-knowledge also helps people make the dozens of smaller, spontaneous decisions that can invest the entire holiday season with special meaning. In the case of Jim, a salesman and the father of three children, a keen awareness of his values enabled him to make a spur-of-the-moment decision that made all the difference in his appreciation of the holiday.

In early December, when Jim was driving his family home from a school crafts fair, he stopped the car so a bent old man could cross the street. Jim watched the man's slow progress for a moment and then made a quick decision. Without saying a word he pulled the car over to the curb, reached for a package of cookies he had bought at the fair, jumped out of the car, and ran after the old man.

As Jim overtook him, the old man became alarmed. He wheeled around and drew back his fist, as if trying to defend himself. Jim quickly said that he wasn't going to hurt him. When the man realized that Jim had something to give him, his eyes filled with tears and he asked Jim why he was giving him a present. Jim was surprised to hear himself say, "Because it's Christmas and I love you." As the old man accepted the cookies, Jim felt tears coming to his eyes, too. "I was overcome with emotion for this stranger," he told us. "That moment captured the true meaning of Christmas for me."

Jim learned that a spontaneous act of generosity to a stranger was what he needed in order to feel more spiritually alive at Christmas. Although this kind of encounter wouldn't be satisfying to everyone, many of the people we talk to say that they feel better about Christmas when they find some way to reach out to others. The challenge is to learn which avenues of expression are most likely to give them the satisfaction they are looking for. Some people feel comfortable writing a check to a favorite charity, while others show their concern by spending time with a sick friend or a lonely relative. People have their own ways of reaching spiritual fulfillment.

Most people find satisfaction at Christmas in traditional ways. They come to feel connected to other people by celebrating with family and friends, get spiritual fulfillment from going to church, and express their generosity and goodwill by donating money to charities and exchanging gifts. These traditions connect them to past Christmases, to other people, and to important ideas and values. And they give them a sense of identity and harmony as well as pleasure.

But we've been surprised at how many people get spiritual rewards at Christmas in highly individual ways. For example, a friend of ours said that his most meaningful Christmas had been spent in the mountains with his wife. A middle-aged woman told us that she had enjoyed Christmas most the year she attended the Christmas services of three different denominations, discovering the common themes in all the sermons. And a woman that we met at a conference told us that she had found the feeling of family she was looking for by adopting an old woman in a nursing home as her children's grandmother and inviting her into their home every Christmas.

It's important to realize that many of the rare moments of joy that light up the holiday cannot be programmed or prescribed. They come as gifts. An unexpected phone call from someone you love, a child's heartfelt generosity, the spontaneous happiness that comes over you in a room smelling of evergreens and glowing with candles, a fresh Christmas snowfall, a feeling of harmony with the world around you—these things cannot be manufactured. But when people are clear about their values at Christmas and find meaningful ways to express them, they've laid the foundations of a soul-satisfying celebration.

In the pages that follow, you will find a values exercise that will help you clarify what's most important to you at Christmas. And then you can read answers to some specific questions people have about how to express their values.

Exercise

WHAT ARE YOU CELEBRATING?

In general, people ask Christmas to do too many things for them. They want it to strengthen their family bonds, give their spirits a lift in the dark days of winter, stimulate their compassion and generosity, help them keep tabs on far-flung friends, confirm their deepest religious beliefs, show off their skills as hosts and hostesses, establish their rank in the social order . . . the list goes on and on. No one celebration can do it all.

This values-clarification exercise will help you decide which parts of Christmas are most deserving of your efforts. Once you have decided that, you will be able to plan a celebration that is in harmony with your deepest beliefs and expressive of who you are as an individual.

To complete the exercise, read through the following ten value statements on the next page, cross off those that have no importance to you, and add any equally important ones that we have not included. Then decide which of the remaining values is most important to you. Put a 1 beside that sentence. Then find the one that is next important to you and put a 2 beside it. Continue in this manner until each statement has been assigned a different number. Even a value that has a low priority can still be important to you. Remember: 1 is highest and 10 is lowest.

- ☆ Christmas is a time to be a peacemaker, within my family and the world at large.
- ☆ Christmas is a time to enjoy being with my immediate family.
- ☆ Christmas is a time to create a beautiful home environment.
- ☆ Christmas is a time to celebrate the birth of Christ.
- ☆ Christmas is a time to exchange gifts with my family and friends.
- ☆ Christmas is a time for parties, entertaining, and visits with friends.
- ☆ Christmas is a time to help those who are less fortunate.
- ☆ Christmas is a time to strengthen bonds with my relatives.
- ☆ Christmas is a time to strengthen my church community.
- ☆ Christmas is a time to take a few days off from work and have a good time.

Questions and Answers

Question 1: *The most important thing to me about Christmas is its promise of peace on earth. What can I do at this time of year to further the cause of world peace?*

Answer: An increasing number of people are looking for ways to make "Peace on Earth, Goodwill Toward Men" more than just a message on their annual Christmas cards. One way to act on your concern is to redirect some of the money you've set aside for holiday expenses to a peace organization. You could make a donation, subscribe to a peace newsletter or magazine, volunteer your time, or give a gift donation or subscription. If you are a member of a church, your denomination undoubtedly has its own peace program. Or you may want to contribute to a national organization. Here are five of the best-known groups:

American Friends Service Committee (AFSC)
Founded in 1917 by the Society of Friends, AFSC tries to encourage and support human survival by working for the abolition of war. In order to achieve this goal, it seeks a nonviolent world order based on global justice and a more equitable sharing of the world's resources. To make a donation or to volunteer your time, write to: The American Friends Service Committee, 1501 Cherry St., Philadelphia, PA 19102.

Fellowship of Reconciliation (FOR)
"FOR is a company of men and women who have a vision of and a commitment to the creation of a peaceful, just world community with full dignity and freedom for every human being." FOR was organized in England in 1914 when an English Quaker and a German Lutheran pastor pledged to remain friends and continue to work for peace, even though their countries were at war. While most of the members of FOR are Christians, the participation of people of Jewish faith and other religious traditions is encouraged. If you would like to make a Christmas contribution to FOR, send a check to: FOR, Box 271, Nyack, NY 10960. FOR publishes a magazine called *Fellowship* eight times a year that keeps readers informed of ongoing peace activities and contains thought-provoking articles on issues relating to peace. A subscription is ten dollars.

New Call to Peacemaking
New Call to Peacemaking is a cooperative effort by the historic peace churches (the Quakers, Mennonites, and Brethren) to strengthen and redirect local church members into an active peace witness. Although much of its activity has focused on

these three churches, it is energetically pursuing peace activities with other churches on the local level. By making a contribution of five dollars or more, you can receive the newsletter *Call to Peacemaking.* The address is: New Call to Peacemaking, Box 1245, Elkhart, Indiana 46515.

Women's Action for Nuclear Disarmament (WAND)
Started in 1980 by Dr. Helen Caldicott, Women's Action for Nuclear Disarmament is a political action committee seeking to mobilize women nationwide in a campaign for international disarmament and the establishment of a Department of Peace within the government. At present there are sixty-five affiliated groups around the country and a mailing list of twenty-two thousand people. Membership dues are ten dollars for students and those on fixed incomes, twenty dollars for individuals, and twenty-five dollars for families. Write to: WAND, 691 Massachusetts Ave., Arlington, MA 02174.

Women's International League for Peace and Freedom (WILPF)
WILPF is the nation's oldest women's peace organization. While its efforts focus on peace programs for women, it is currently involved in a nationwide effort to register a million people who believe in calling a halt to the nuclear arms race. When you become a member, you automatically receive the magazine *Peace Freedom,* which is published nine times a year. Family memberships are thirty dollars per year and individual memberships are twenty-five dollars. WILPF also sells posters, T-shirts, Christmas cards, and gift memberships that could be used as Christmas presents. The address is: WILPF, 1213 Race St., Philadelphia, PA 19107.

Question 2: *I feel strongly that I have an obligation to my church at Christmas, but so often I get stretched too thin. I end up feel-*

ing exhausted and depleted instead of renewed by my obligations. What can I do?

Answer: Because we talk with so many committed church people about Christmas, we know how common the problem of burnout is. It seems almost axiomatic that a few capable, energetic people carry most of the responsibility of church activities. As one church leader told us, "If you want to get something done, ask someone who is already busy."

The first step in getting control of your church commitments during November and December is to sit down with a blank piece of paper and a calendar and try to get a good idea of how busy you are likely to be. Write on the calendar any non-Christmas church activities that will probably occur during the season (include regular committee meetings, social events, children's activities, and so on). If you don't know the dates, write the items on the piece of paper under the heading "Ongoing Church Commitments." Next, write down any work or social commitments that you know about (include dinner meetings, out-of-town trips, bridge groups). If you don't know when they will occur, put them under the heading "Work and Social Commitments." Finally, do the same for your family Christmas activities. Although many of these activities will be hard to place on the calendar (such as baking cookies with the kids, mailing packages, shopping for special groceries), try to pin down as many of them as possible on specific days. The rest can go on your paper under the heading "Family Activities." At this point, you will have a pretty good idea of what your schedule will look like this holiday season, and you will know how many other church responsibilities you can comfortably take on.

The second step is to determine what obligations at church you would like to add, if any. One way to do this is to run over in your mind the jobs that will likely have to be done and ask yourself if you feel drawn toward any of them. Another way is to discern which needs call out for your attention by considering them in prayer. To help you determine which needs you should be meeting, you might ask yourself: (1) What is my motivation for committing to this project? Is it guilt, pride, a desire for recognition? Often these emotions are not sufficient to carry you through the course of a project in the spirit of serenity and enthusiasm you desire. (2) If I take on this obligation, will I be so tightly scheduled that I won't have time to rest, relax, or respond spontaneously to some important opportunity that may come up later? We have been impressed by how often those precious moments of fulfillment at Christmas occur in the blank spaces around scheduled events, when you have time to reflect on your experiences and deepen your understanding.

If you are a church leader, you are probably well aware of the oversize load carried by a few people in your congregation at Christmas. Keep this problem in mind when you are thinking of people to fill particular positions. Perhaps your church could make it a practice to seek out good potential leaders and consciously prepare them for responsibility. In many cases, asking people to take on work for the church at Christmas can be a ministry to them. People you know to be lonely or shy or unsure can gain added confidence and much needed social interaction in the process of working for the church. Although many jobs must be done by the most competent person available, others are not so crucial. If you can afford to let the job be done less than perfectly, then ask the people who need to be asked and concentrate your attention on the benefits they are getting, rather than on how the end product looks.

In addition, you may want to consider, with the church community, whether all the activities and events you have scheduled at Christmas really further your ministry or whether they add busyness without adding depth and meaning. The Appendix will give you additional suggestions for effective church programming at Christmas.

When you have considered ahead of time, through prayer and systematic thought, which commitments you are called to take on, you will feel equally confident in saying yes or no when asked. Perhaps the best advice we have read on this subject comes from an essay in the December 1891 *Ladies' Home Journal:*

> It has always seemed to me the most difficult of problems to combine in daily life the two parts of the Christmas motto; for the effort to show "goodwill toward men" is only too apt to destroy the "peace," and to make home an uncomfortable place where several over-worked people sleep, eat, and discuss plans. Words written by John Foster early in this century often come to my mind. "If I had the power," he says, "of touching a large part of mankind with a spell, amid all this inane activity, it should be this short sentence, Be Quiet, Be Quiet." Surely home life would be happier and philanthropy more helpful if we would but let the peace of Christ rule in our hearts, and learn that rest is not selfishness, and bustling overwork no true service.

Question 3: *I don't have the time or money to get involved in charity work at Christmas, but I would like my celebration to be less self-serving. What are some simple ways I can help others at Christmas?*

Answer: Acts of charity don't have to be dramatic departures from your normal routine, or cost money, or take a lot of extra time and effort. One of the simplest and most satisfying ways to benefit others without changing your celebration too much is to buy your gifts from charitable organizations. When you purchase your gifts from church bazaars, third-world craft organizations, indigenous craftsmen, or nonprofit agencies, you are giving a double gift—one to the person who unwraps it on Christmas morning, and one to the charitable organization itself. For a list of national and international charitable organizations that offer Christmas gifts for sale, see page 214.

* * *

Question 4: *I don't feel comfortable becoming involved in institutional charities. What are some other simple ways I can reach out to people?*

Answer: Many people find great satisfaction in initiating acts of kindness within their own circle of family members and friends. Just being especially thoughtful to the people you see all the time can make a difference.

First, ask yourself which person or family that you know would most appreciate some personal contact with you during the season. A walk, a shared meal, a phone call, a letter, some free time while you take over their normal responsibilities, a compliment—all these simple things make the ideal of goodwill come alive at Christmas.

Second, you might ask yourself what nonmaterial gift each member of your family would most appreciate from you this Christmas. Perhaps your spouse would like you to be more relaxed or more involved with him or her; your mother might appreciate it if you were a more attentive listener; your father might welcome it if you paid special attention to one of his interests; and your children would undoubtedly be excited at the prospect of more quiet time alone with you. The possibilities for reaching out to the people around you in quiet, simple ways are endless.

Question 5: *I would like to do something helpful in my own community at Christmas, but I don't know what. How can I get involved?*

Answer: There are many ways to get directly involved with the needy in your own area at Christmas. The organization that comes immediately to mind is the Salvation Army, which itself is practically a Christmas tradition. For many people, the Christmas season doesn't really begin until they hear the familiar sound of the bell ringer. Although the Salvation Army is active all year long, most of their good works are done during the holidays, when they depend on volunteers and donations to accomplish their goals. During a typical Christmas season, the Salvation Army delivers festive meals to shut-ins and poor people; donates gifts to children; gives Christmas parties in needy neighborhoods; and serves meals to transients, patients in alcoholic-treatment centers, and the families of prisoners.

These special Christmas activities, and the ongoing counseling services they provide in the areas of household budgeting and management and employment possibilities, depend on volunteers. If you want to get involved in any of these activities, call your local Salvation Army office, or write to the national headquarters: The Salvation Army, 120 West 14th St., New York, NY 10011.

Many other local groups will also be involved in helping people in your community at Christmas. The director of volunteer services at your local hospital will give you information on the ways you can help medical patients. Or you can contact your local police and fire departments, Boy Scout and Girl Scout offices, Lions Club, Volunteers of America, neighborhood church, or United Way office. Many communities also have volunteer bureaus that match those who need help at Christmas with those who can give it.

Question 6: *I have always wanted to visit a nursing home at Christmas, but I don't know how to go about it. Can you help?*

Answer: First, we should say that not everyone is well suited for nursing home visits. If the thought upsets you, or you feel uncomfortable around older people, there are many other ways to serve. But if you really think you would enjoy such a visit, here are some suggestions to make your visit a success.

☆ Rest assured that one visit is better than none. Even if you can't come regularly, your presence will be appreciated at Christmas.

☆ Let the nursing home staff know you are coming, so they can coordinate visits and prepare the patients. If possible, visit the nursing home on Christmas Eve or Christmas Day, since this is when it is most painful for the patients to be alone.

☆ When you visit, don't be in a hurry. Most patients have time on their hands, and your visit will probably seem too short no matter how long you stay.

☆ Do bring your children. The chance to be around young people is a treat. Children and animals do more to cheer up older people than almost anything else. (You may want to prepare your children for the visit by telling them what to expect.)

☆ If you are lucky enough to have the time and opportunity to develop a continuing relationship with an older person in a nursing home, remember that one of the best gifts you can give is the gift of expectation. Old people often have nothing to look forward to. One woman told us that she had adopted a man in a nursing home and always made it a point to let him know in advance when she would be visiting. That way, he had the pleasure of anticipating her arrival in addition to the pleasure of her company.

☆ After you have developed a friendship with a patient, consider bringing a tape recorder to record his or her life story. One woman told us she did this and typed up the resulting "biography" for her older friend's family.

☆ If you want to bring gifts, remember to provide some for both men and women, wrap each gift and attach a card indicating which sex it is for, and take the gifts to the front desk to ask the receptionist how they should be distributed. Here are some gift ideas:

Live flowers
Useful gifts such as lap robes, bags for personal belongings, slippers, bibs, pillows, sweaters

Books with large print
An outside excursion to a park or restaurant or the local shops, if the older person is mobile
A deck of cards or other game that you can play together
Volunteer to mount an older person's family photographs in an album

Do *not* bring candy or cookies without the permission of the nursing home staff. Many older patients are diabetic.

***Question** 7: I would like to donate money to charity, but I'm not sure whom to give to. How can I find out?*

Answer: If you are shorter on time than on money, or if you aren't comfortable with face-to-face contact with the people you are helping, writing a check and sending it to a worthy cause can make you feel good, and donations are vital to the operation of most nonprofit charitable organizations. According to Helen O'Rourke, vice-president of the Council of Better Business Bureaus, fifty-three billion dollars was donated to charity in this country in 1981. Ninety percent of it was given by individuals, and the remaining 10 percent was split evenly between foundations and corporations.

If a national agency looks like a good charity to you, but you want to be sure that it is legitimate and effective, the National Information Bureau can help you find out. The NIB is a nonprofit, independent watchdog organization that evaluates charitable agencies according to certain standards of ideals and performance. Although it doesn't usually report on local, religious, fraternal, or political organizations, it does issue reports on agencies with programs in fields such as animal protection, conservation, education, health, youth, international relief and development, legal defense, minorities, and social welfare. For more information, call 212-532-8595, or write to: The National Information Bureau, 419 Park Ave. South, New York, NY 10016.

☆

CHAPTER 7:

A Simple Christmas

You are riding through the snowy New England countryside in a sleigh pulled by a matched team of Clydesdale horses. The only sounds you hear are the footfalls of the horses, the creaking of harnesses, and the ringing of sleigh bells. Your cheeks are red from the rush of cold air, but the wool blankets heaped around you keep you snug and warm. As much as you are enjoying this ride, you are also eager to reach the warm, brightly lit home in the country where you are expected for Christmas dinner. The country is so beautiful, and your spirits are so high, that you start humming "I'll Be Home for Christmas" in time to the jingling of the bells.

You finally arrive at your destination, and as you knock on the door of the elegant country house, a television announcer breaks into your reverie. All of a sudden you realize that you are sitting in an armchair watching television, not riding in a horse-drawn sleigh, and that this delightful sixty-second ride through the snow has been brought to you by a certain brand of beer. As the commercial fades away, you are faced once again with the reality of everyday life.

The admen who conceived this commercial know what people really want for Christmas. Most people long for a celebration that is just as serene, connected to the natural world, and free of modern distractions as this idyllic sleigh ride through the country. But the fact is, most people are caught up in a labyrinth of holiday plans and projects: there are gifts to buy, packages to mail, cookies to bake, homes to decorate, choir rehearsals to attend, travel plans to make. Many people are so busy that the only time they get out of doors is those few seconds it takes to dash from the house to the car. And their chance for a peaceful celebration is overwhelmed by factors they can't seem to control.

We get a clear picture of how people really want Christmas to be when we ask workshop participants to spend a few minutes fantasizing a perfect holiday. We ask them to imagine what the celebration would be like if they could throw out all their old ideas and habits and start anew with only their personal tastes and preferences to take into account. The only requirement is that they imagine the Christmas that makes them feel most fulfilled.

The fantasies people create turn out to be filled with unique and colorful details. One person will imagine Christmas in the Alps. Another will camp on the beach. Someone else will stay at home but change his everyday environment by unplugging the television and the phone. But the most startling thing about all of the fantasies is that, underneath the eccentric details, most of them are essentially alike. Despite the fact that we urge everyone to give his imagination free reign, nearly everyone comes up with a variation of the same celebration. We have discovered that most people are united by a single Christmas dream. In brief outline, it goes like this:

Snow is falling in a quiet and serene natural setting. Inside the house, a fire glows in the fireplace. There are few modern distractions like televisions, telephones, cars, or radios, and the only holiday decorations are a Christmas tree, candles, greens, and simple homemade decorations. Christmas presents, if there are any, are inexpensive remembrances, or intangible spiritual gifts. The family members are in a good mood and enjoy each other's company in simple ways, like taking walks or sleigh rides together, or gathering around the fire to sing carols or play musical instruments. It doesn't take much to make people laugh, and if there is work to be done, such as the preparation of traditional food, the tasks are shared or completed in some magical way without effort. The children are happy and well behaved and enjoy each other's company. A relaxed, loving atmosphere washes over everyone and awakens them to all the religious or spiritual possibilities that unite them at Christmas.

In this fantasy, there are no elaborate Christmas centerpieces, exotically decorated trees, tables set with Spode Christmas china, or three-hour gift-unwrapping sessions. Most of the activities that require a lot of money and preparation have vanished, so people have the peace of mind to be receptive to each other and the world around them. This universal dream shows that at Christmas people want to be in harmony with the natural world, be united with friends and relatives, be filled with a spirit of love and acceptance, and have their everyday cares lightened with fun and laughter.

This leads us to an obvious question. If most people are longing for such a simple celebration, why are their holidays so complicated? Why don't more people pare down their activities and obligations until they have the peaceful, spontaneous celebration they envision?

To begin with, there are two factors that stand in the way. First, most people's fantasies involve a little magic. As soon as they close their eyes, they suddenly become the proud owners of a home in the country complete with a fireplace, a sleigh, and a ready team of horses. Or they wake up in the morning blessed with a fresh Christmas snowfall. Fantasies, by their very nature, involve a lot of wishful thinking. And fantasies can't serve as blueprints until they're ruthlessly pruned of all the make-believe.

Second, people cleverly screen out life's unpleasant realities in their fantasies. No one has ever described a fantasy to us in which they had to cope with crying babies, bored teen-agers, dirty dishes, or complicated negotiations over who should pay for what. Even the simplest Christmas involves some planning and rearranging of schedules, but no one ever mentions any of these wearisome details. People have an understandable wish to be like children at Christmas, with all of the fun and none of the responsibilities.

But wishful thinking aside, the core of the fantasy—simple gifts, natural decorations, a fire, traditional food, leisurely schedules, music, time spent out of doors, an emphasis on family activities—is well within reach. And we're meeting a lot of people who are moving in this direction. But there are many more who still feel trapped in an expensive, commercial, and complicated Christmas.

Part of the reason more people aren't living out their Christmas dreams is that everywhere they turn they are encouraged to make Christmas as expensive and elaborate and busy as possible. TV commercials show excited children coming downstairs on Christmas morning to a tree heaped with goodies. Magazines urge mom to make this Christmas one her family will remember by filling the house with lavish decorations. Dads are told to be grateful they have credit cards so they can go into debt to give their families the Christmas they really deserve. The number of days until Christmas is printed in big type on the front pages of newspapers just to make sure everyone is aware of the countdown. The implication is that there's so much to do and buy that everyone must rush to get everything done on time.

Why don't newspapers and magazines and commercials tell people simply to relax and enjoy the holiday? It's not hard to figure out. If everyone decorated with greens, gave token presents to the immediate family only, gathered together for a potluck dinner, and posted a handful of seasonal letters, our national economy would have to make a big adjustment. A simple Christmas is an economic bust.

But it's not just economic pressure that's been keeping Christmas complex. Even while people want to simplify Christmas, they may also have a strong need to keep Christmas the same. Especially when their lives are stressful and subject to change, they want Christmas to be a haven of familiar rituals. And most people today grew up with fairly elaborate celebrations. Even though part of them would like Christmas to be simpler and less commercial, they also want to hold on to the comfort and nostalgia of their childhood Christmases.

Others find that family obligations stand in the way. In their fantasies, most people feel complete freedom to pick and choose from the family roster the group of relatives they want to spend Christmas with. And, of course, in their daydreams, everyone on this handpicked list goes along with their plans. In real life, it's not that simple. For example, a woman named Hillary told us that her husband's parents were ailing and counted on her a great deal to help them out at Christmas. She and her husband spent many days helping clean and decorate their house, going shopping for them, and cheering them up.

Hillary told us that this was not the way she would choose to spend Christmas if she had only her own wishes to consider. When she imagined a perfect holiday, she saw her family going to the beach or to a mountain cabin. They were all outdoors people and longed to be away from the city and free from the demands of others. Nevertheless, it was more important to her to be accommodating. "My in-laws have no other family," she told us. "We're all they have. And family is what Christmas is all about. I'm glad to do it for them."

But Hillary, like most people, was able to hold on to the spirit of her fantasy Christmas despite her family obligations. She told us that on Christmas Day she was able to leave the grandparents with a cousin and take a long walk in the park with her husband and children. "The park was quiet and empty," she told us, "and we felt as peaceful as if we were in the middle of the woods."

We've met a lot of people, however, who are able to live out their entire holiday fantasies.

This was the case for a sixty-five-year-old woman named Katharine who masterminded a plan to gather three generations of her family together for a simple Christmas celebration at the beach. She saw the need for change when she looked around her one Christmas and saw that most of the family was just going through the motions of having a good time. "Especially the teen-agers," she said. "They were pretty obviously bored with the whole thing." She spent some time after Christmas thinking about what would make her family most happy and decided it was a simple Christmas on the Oregon coast. In the summer, Katharine proposed to the family that they combine their Christmas money and rent a cabin at the beach for the coming holiday. She suggested that they not exchange gifts and simplify the cooking by bringing along precooked potluck dishes. Everyone in the family was excited by the idea, and someone even suggested that they bring along materials to make ornaments for a tree.

Despite the fact that Katharine was the one who came up with the idea of not exchanging gifts, she told us that she got two beautiful Christmas presents all the same. One was the fact that a grandson took her for a walk on the beach to tell her it was the best Christmas of his life. And the other was waking up on Christmas morning, looking out the window, and seeing that her grandchildren had written MERRY CHRISTMAS GRANDMA in ten-foot letters in the sand.

Katharine and her family discovered that even dramatically simplifying their celebration did not take away any of its value. In fact, they all agreed it was the best Christmas they had ever spent together. No one was burdened with long hours in the kitchen. All of them had time to relax and talk in depth with each other. And while they had been worried at first about how Christmas would feel without gifts, they felt relieved to be free from all the worry and expense of gift-giving.

Whether you live out your Christmas dream in every detail or find one small part to incorporate, taking the time to create the fantasy is one of the most important steps you can take. Your fantasies give you a new enthusiasm for Christmas and the sense of direction you need to start building a better celebration.

In the following exercise, you will have a chance to visualize the kind of Christmas *you* really want. Then we will answer typical questions people have when they're thinking about simplifying their celebrations. In addition, the Appendix offers specific suggestions for simplifying your decorations, Christmas cards, entertaining, gift-giving, and food preparation.

EXERCISE

A CHRISTMAS FANTASY

The following fantasy exercise will give you a clearer idea of what you are really looking for in Christmas. When you are through reading these instructions, close your eyes and imagine Christmas two years from now. We have chosen this length of time because it's far enough away to give you some distance from your current celebration, but not so far away that a lot of your circumstances will have changed.

When you are ready to begin, choose a quiet location where you won't be interrupted for ten or fifteen minutes. Imagine any kind of Christmas you wish as long as it is deeply satisfying. You can confine your fantasy to Christmas proper, or include the whole season. It may be very much like your present celebration or entirely different. You can magically include your favorite friends and relatives and make them behave any way you wish. You can celebrate in any setting. You don't have to keep a single traditional Christmas activity, or you can keep them all. This will be Christmas the way you have always wanted it to be.

As you begin to fantasize, there will probably be a jumble of possibilities competing for your attention. If you find yourself with multiple fantasies, keep returning to the ideas that make you feel most satisfied.

Once you have settled on a particular fantasy, stick with it until you have enriched it with lots of details. Imagine the physical setting, the activities, how you are feeling, and how other people are feeling. What kind of food is there? How was it made? Are there any gifts? What are they like?

When you have completed your fantasy, write it down on a separate sheet (or sheets) of paper. Feel free to elaborate as you write. Then answer these questions:

1. Of all the ways your fantasy was different from your usual celebration, which difference was most satisfying to you?
2. Which parts (if any) of your fantasy would be most feasible to actually do next Christmas?

People often get a great deal of pleasure from reading the fantasies of others. Here is a sampling from those we have collected:

> A few days before Christmas, Grace and the kids and I pack *leisurely* and go up to a mountain cabin. The roads are packed with snow but surprisingly drivable. The kids don't know where we're going, but Grace does, and she's *relaxed.* We talk. We talk about some things past and some things future. Then we arrive at a comfortable, real log cabin in a pine forest.
>
> The kids are excited but well behaved. We unload and settle in in no time flat. There are no hassles getting the kids fed or getting them to take a nap. We are all relaxed.
>
> The next few days pass in wonderful, calm togetherness. Romps in the snow. Wonderful but not overstuffed meals. Then on Christmas Eve we all bundle up and go to a nearby town for a midnight Christmas service. The kids fall asleep in our arms and are perfect angels. The service is calm, peaceful, hopeful, and full of Christmas music.

In the morning Ben and Margaret drive up to spend the day. Both sets of kids are overjoyed to see each other but are still well behaved. My mother-in-law arrives later in the day. Football on TV. A turkey in the oven. Rest. Joy. Fellowship.

* * *

For my perfect Christmas we would go and live in a log cabin at the beginning of December. It would be snowing and we would travel by sleigh. We would cut down our own tree and have no electricity. For Christmas my mom and dad would get me my own horse and I would go off riding by myself in the snow.

The days would be cold and clear and the snow would not melt for a long time. We would make our own ornaments and have hardwood floors. We would have wheat, corn, eggs, and other things and we would live there until school started again.

* * *

My perfect Christmas would happen by accident. Nobody would even know it was Christmas. All my family would happen to converge on a big house in a good mood with a few days to spend together.

It would be nobody's home, so no one person would feel responsible for cleaning and decorating it or fixing it up for company. We'd all go for a walk in the woods and bring evergreen boughs and holly back to the house because we liked the smells. And because there's no electricity, the house would glow with candlelight.

Someone would have brought a special bottle of red wine, and we'd sit down to a simple but wonderful meal. We'd be in such a relaxed and open mood, and would have had such a good day walking in the woods, that someone would propose a toast and say, "This is such a fine day, it feels just like Christmas." Then we'd all smile and clink our glasses together, feeling warm and together.

There would be no talk of Jesus, but we would be very loving and accepting of ourselves and each other. For the first time we would have the sensation of seeing each other at our best.

In the morning, we'd wake up to a snowy day. No one had expected this snowfall, and even the weather report hadn't predicted it. It was a gift. And as we sat around having a late and relaxed breakfast, someone would rush to his suitcase with something he had brought for another person—not a wrapped present, just something he thought the other person would enjoy: a special book, a drawing, a new recipe . . . There would be something for everyone.

A day later, we'd all take a final, exhilarating walk in the snowy woods. And then all would pack up and go home, never knowing that it was Christmas, but feeling happy and at peace.

Questions and Answers

Question 1: *I'm realizing that I'd like our Christmas to be a lot simpler than it is. How do I go about making changes?*

Answer: Reading this book has probably suggested to you one or two important changes you would like to make in your celebration. You may already have in mind a few specific alterations, but if you don't, review your answers to the questions following the fantasy exercise. In the pages that follow we will show you how to make a written plan incorporating the changes you would most like to make. If you are the kind of person who does not like structured planning, here are some general recommendations.

You may have been celebrating Christmas in more or less the same way for years. There's a certain comfort in this familiarity even if your celebration is not totally satisfying. So we advise that you proceed slowly. It might help you to look upon next Christmas as the first year in a five-year plan. Then you will have the patience to make small initial changes.

Concentrate on changes that you can make by yourself or for which you know you have family support. There's no point in initiating a change that will meet with opposition. For example, if you do not have the same religious views as your spouse, putting your energy into creating new religious rituals for the family may be counterproductive. Concentrating on your own spiritual life will probably be much more rewarding.

Remember that you do not have to make visible changes in your celebration to feel better about it. Many of the people we've talked to report dramatic improvements in their feelings about Christmas just through lowering their expectations for their own performance or going about their traditional activities in a more relaxed way.

***Question** 2: I would like to make a written plan for next Christmas. How do I go about it?*

Answer: We encourage people to take the time to set specific, written goals for the holiday because a plan helps them focus their thoughts and gives them added incentive for carrying out their ideas.

First, as you make your plan, you should realize that this blueprint will not be your only instrument of change. You will probably find yourself making numerous small adjustments in your celebration that are too insignificant to mention in your plan. All of these moment-by-moment decisions will add up to a more enjoyable celebration. Your plan is merely a tool to help you focus on the important changes you wish to make.

Second, set small and specific goals. Our experience has shown us that people need time to adjust to new ideas—especially in an area of their lives where traditions play such an important role. Therefore, modest plans tend to be most successful. Besides, most people find that they don't want to change all that much about the way they celebrate Christmas. More often, they just want to clear away a few activities that have lost meaning, add a tradition or two, and look for more depth and spirit in their established rituals.

Third, the time of year when you are making this plan is going to play a key role in determining your goals. If you are planning in midsummer, you have the time to make changes that involve a lot of people, such as talking to all family members about giving fewer or simpler gifts. If you are making your plan a week before Christmas, you need to set your sights on changes that can be enacted at the last minute, such as adding a new family activity the day after Christmas that will help your children gradually wind down from all the excitement.

Fourth, as we have said before, you will have greater success if you focus on goals that you can accomplish independently, or that have the likely support of everyone involved. For example, if you are bothered by a relative's excessive drinking, you will probably be frustrated if you define your goal this way: "I would like to encourage my father to drink less this Christmas." A more realistic goal statement would be "I would like to add activities to our celebration that would take the emphasis off drinking." This second goal is one that you could accomplish even without your father's cooperation.

The first step in actually making your written Christmas plan is to bring to mind your most important ideas for change. Take out a sheet of paper and list those ideas.

Next, select two or three of the most important and realistic ideas to incorporate this season. How do you make this choice? We have found that the fantasy exercise often gives people the best indication of what's most important to them about Christmas. You may also find it helpful to ask yourself these questions:

1. If my goals involve other family members, am I likely to have their support?

2. Do I have the time and resources to accomplish these goals this year?
3. Will fulfilling these goals keep intact all the parts of my celebration that have strong emotional appeal to me and others?

If you answered yes to all three of these questions, chances are you have realistic goals. If you found some difficulties, stop to revise your goals before going on to the next step.

For some examples of good goal sentences, look through this list that we collected at the end of one of our workshops:

☆ I want more help with the Christmas preparations.
☆ I want to feel more relaxed this holiday season.
☆ I want to simplify my gift-giving.
☆ I want to spend more relaxed time with my children this Christmas.
☆ I want to give less commercial gifts.

When you have two or three workable goals, your next step is to decide exactly how you're going to reach them. So far, you may only have a general idea of what you're aiming for. Look at your goals and think of one, two, or three activities that will help you accomplish them. Remember that unless you are assured of other people's cooperation, it's best to focus on activities that you can do by yourself.

Next you need to describe these activities in simple written sentences. These sentences should tell you exactly *what* you are going to do and *when* it should be done. Here is an example:

Goal: I want to simplify my gift-giving.

Activity 1: I will write letters to Aunt Carol and Aunt Rebecca suggesting that we give gifts only to the children and mail those letters by October 1.

Activity 2: I will talk with my friends at work this week and suggest that we go out to lunch together instead of exchanging Christmas presents.

Activity 3: I will do all of my gift-shopping for the children from the Childcraft catalog and phone in the order by the end of October.

When you have finished choosing activities for all of your goals and checked to make sure they are small and specific, have family support, and are fixed in a specific time frame, you are through. You may want to keep your plan tacked up on the refrigerator or on the bulletin board, where you will be reminded of it and you can cross off each activity as it's completed.

Question 3: *Now that I have a plan, how do I share it with my family?*

Answer: You, of course, are the best judge of how to approach your family. You may have relatives who are likely to be supportive of all your ideas and will only require a quick phone call to fill them in on all the details. On the other hand, you may have family members who will need to hear your reasons for seeking change and then have time to think about it. Only you know which is the case.

But we do have some general recommendations for talking to family members about making changes. First, choose your time carefully. Wait until other people are in a relaxed and accepting frame of mind before you launch into your ideas. Second, be nonthreatening. Unless the other family members have done a lot of thinking about Christmas, introduce the topic gently. Third, take the time to explain your reasons for wanting to make changes. Once people know the sincere motivations behind your plan, they are usually more supportive. And finally, talk to others as soon as possible. Many people like to plan for Christmas early.

☆

CHAPTER 8:

Christmas Revival

When people in our workshops describe their visions of a perfect Christmas, we usually hear wonderfully detailed fantasies—a ski trip in the Rockies, a country Christmas in Vermont, or delightful variations on specific family rituals. But one woman was able to capture her dream for a better Christmas in just a few words. "I have only one request," she said, "and that's for Christmas to bring my family closer together. I want us to have fun together, not sit in separate corners of the room reading magazines or watching TV." As she said this, she stretched her arms out to her sides and then slowly brought them together in a big circle, as if to gather up her scattered family.

As she explained her wish, she told us that every Christmas her family went through the same sterile routine. "On Christmas Eve, I'm in the kitchen cooking while everyone else is reading magazines or watching TV. Then we eat. Then a few people help me clean up and it's back to the television. The next morning, we open the gifts. Then I cook breakfast. The dishes are cleaned up. And then it's more TV and sports magazines. Then I'm back in the kitchen again, cooking dinner."

This bleak portrayal of a family Christmas is all too familiar to us. Many of the people that we've talked to spend their holiday opening gifts, sitting, talking, eating, drinking, listening to other people sing, watching other people play ball games on TV, and watching television specials. At times, it seems as if we, as a nation, have lost the art of celebrating.

Our passive American way of Christmas seems even more flat and empty when we compare it to the lively folk festivals of other countries. For example, in one workshop, a man named José who had recently emigrated from Mexico volunteered to tell us about his childhood Christmas. Most of his memories centered on Los Posados, the Mexican Christmas festival that reenacts Joseph and Mary's search for an inn and lasts from December 16 until Christmas Day. José explained that on each of the nine nights of the celebration, a different family invited the villagers in for an evening of singing, treats, and a chance to break a *piñata.*

José had especially fond memories of the last night of the festival, when his female relatives gathered in one kitchen to make *tamales* and traditional Mexican sweets. As soon as the food was ready, the whole neighborhood got together and partied until daybreak. "There was dancing and drinks for the adults and hot punch and games for the kids," he said. When he was through, we asked how the American Christmas seemed to him, and José answered that it looked pretty sad. Every holiday he wished he could fly his family back to Mexico. "In Mexico, we had Christmas," he said. "In the United States, you just have presents."

Our modern version of Christmas seems just as uninspired when compared to celebrations of the past. In Victorian England, for example, families celebrated Christmas with an exuberant collection of games—blindman's buff, charades, snapdragon, and hunt the slipper—where *all* family members took part, not just the children. You can sense their joy in the following excerpts from *The Victorian Christmas Book* by Anthony and Peter Miall (New York: Pantheon Books, 1978): "A speckled physician of sixty sitting on his hams on a carpet, and passing the slipper under him, with all the dexterity, if not with all the glee, of a school boy, is a sight to be enjoyed."

After the games and elaborate, full-costume charades, there

were conjuring tricks, recitations, and singing. And then came the dancing: "Hark! the sound of music: the Christmas dance begins; and Polka—the universal polka—summons all hands and feet to another celebration; and to a sport in comparison to which all others are of small account."

The vitality of the English family Christmas was equaled by the celebrations of early Americans. A hundred years ago, our great-grandparents spent their Christmas vacations sleighing, skating, caroling, and masquerading, and when they came inside with red cheeks and high spirits, they played parlor games or rolled back the carpets and invited the neighbors over for a dance. Here is a description of a multigenerational Christmas party that appeared in the December 1895 *Good Housekeeping*:

> Each Christmas we'd converge on a long, wide cheerful farm house kitchen and play games like "wade the swamp," "keep post office," "pick grapes," "measure tape" and "hiss cat."
>
> Sometimes we danced, with the fiddlers perched high on kitchen tables. There was no mincing along on one's toes with every step "just so." . . . We "swung our pardners" as partners are not often swung, sometimes lifting them quite off their feet. We danced to the good old tunes of "Dan Tucker" and "Money-musk" and we kept it up until "broad day-light in the morning."
>
> There was nothing formal about these affairs. Nothing graceful, nothing "put-on," nothing refined, but those who attended them were genuinely and unaffectedly happy, and Christmas meant much to them.

Learning about the traditions, games, and activities that delighted our ancestors provides clues to the current widespread nostalgia for an old-fashioned Christmas. It's not just the trappings of yesterday's celebrations that people want—prairie dresses for their little girls, Colonial ornaments for their trees, authentic reproductions of sleigh bells for their front doors—it's the very life and spirit of past celebrations that they hunger for. The consumer's, spectator's celebration of today is dreary by comparison. For many of the people we talk to, Christmas is often just a little bit more of the things they are used to all year round—more food, more people, more material goods. But nothing dramatically different. The folk traditions and family activities that added so much mystery and cadence to the holiday have been largely forgotten.

What has happened to them all? As recently as the middle of the nineteenth century, they were intact. All around the country there were pockets of Spanish, German, English, French, Scandinavian, and Dutch Christmas celebrations. In fact, until the late 1800s there was no such thing as a distinct American Christmas. But by the turn of the century, the population had become more integrated, and the various national customs began to merge together.

Because of this amalgamation, a modern family celebration may contain traces of five or six different cultures. A family may decorate the tree with gingerbread cookies like the Germans, have oyster stew on Christmas Eve like the French, have a *piñata* party for the children like the Mexicans, and eat plum pudding for Christmas dinner like the English. There is no doubt that this bountiful inheritance adds vitality to the American Christmas, because it gives people so many wonderful traditions to pick and choose from. But in some ways, the absence of a single body of traditions makes things more difficult, because each family must assume full responsibility for piecing together a coherent celebration. In addition, because each family makes slightly different choices, there's no chance for the communitywide celebrations that bring such joy in countries like Mexico. Ultimately, each family must rely on its own energy and imagination to define its traditions and keep them alive.

With such diluted traditions, and so little reinforcement for preserving them, it's no wonder that the common denominator of

American Christmas celebrations is holiday commercialism. In fact, it could be said that our national celebration begins with the opening ritual of going Christmas shopping the day after Thanksgiving and closes with the hallowed tradition of returning unwanted gifts on December 26. And in between, our citywide observances of Christmas are confined to come-hither "holiday events" in shopping malls.

Families without strong family or ethnic traditions often rely on Christmas commercialism to provide the structure and meaning of their celebrations, depending on an elaborate gift-exchange and the passive consumption of media events for the bulk of their fun and excitement. This was true for a twenty-five-year-old woman named Melissa. For years, the members of her family had focused most of their energy on buying presents for each other, but like many other people, they didn't find this entirely satisfying. "We were sick of all the commercialism," Melissa told us. "Gifts made sense when we were kids, but we were now all adults, so we wanted to do away with some of the trappings." In the fall of 1980, she and her boyfriend, her parents, and her older brother decided to celebrate Christmas by just getting together for a visit and a smorgasbord brunch.

But when Melissa and her family took away the gifts and the elaborate decorations, they found that they had little left. "We had a beautiful meal," Melissa said, "and then went out to the living room to talk. It was pleasant. But we all had the feeling that there was something missing." While they enjoyed each other's company and were relieved not to be overburdened with all the details of gift-giving, the celebration seemed empty. As Melissa told us, "Christmas was an existential abyss."

Many people are eager to eliminate some of the more commercial aspects of their family celebrations, but like Melissa's family, they don't want to end up with a bare-bones Christmas, either. They want a vital and fun-filled celebration that fully measures up to all those weeks of anticipation. They want to let go of parts of Christmas that have little meaning to them, but they also want to find some way to live out the joy and excitement of the holiday season.

What can families do to add to the merriment of their celebrations? By looking to the past, exploring other cultures, and talking with people in this country who have wonderful Christmases, we have learned that there are some simple, inexpensive, and noncommercial ways to enliven the holiday.

One of the first is to make sure that every family member has a vital role to play in the traditions the family already has. People generally take the most pleasure in activities they are really involved in. But all too often, as we pointed out in the earlier chapters, wives and mothers play most of the key roles in the family production while the other family members are passive recipients of all of their labors.

A Portland, Oregon, family found a way to get everyone more involved in the celebration. One year, three adult sisters were discussing their Christmas reunion plans, when one of them suggested that they eliminate the traditional Christmas brunch. In the past, when all three families congregated, it had meant cooking up a meal for eighteen people, and that was a lot of extra work for the women. One of the husbands overheard this proposal and made a mild protest. It just wouldn't be Christmas, he said, without that traditional meal. His wife quickly suggested that the men make the brunch that year. The three husbands got together for a quick consultation and decided to accept the challenge.

That Christmas, when all the gifts had been unwrapped, the three men trooped into the kitchen, closed the door behind them, and started cooking. The women were grateful to have a chance to sit in the living room, play with the children, and admire the presents. Two hours later, the men called everyone into the dining room and presented the family with a beautiful brunch that featured grilled trout and pancakes. The meal was superb and the men's pride was obvious.

The following year, the men decided to make this an annual event. And they got the children involved by asking them to be responsible for setting the table. On their own, the children decided to make a centerpiece, a hand-printed menu, and place cards. By giving the men and children more active roles in the celebration, this family created a fun-filled tradition.

A second step families can take to recapture the spirit of Christmas is to include activities that add movement and physical activity to the celebration. As we've read accounts of past Christmases, we've been struck by how often the holiday was observed with enthusiastic bursts of energy. Whether it was through dancing, mime, parading, or putting on plays, people broke stride with the daily round of work and rest by participating in high-spirited activities that got them all up and moving.

Today, you can find this kind of physical activity in any number of ways at Christmas. You can walk to the store to get that extra pound of butter, or play charades instead of sitting around watching TV. Or you can do something as ambitious as renting a ski lodge in the mountains over Christmas vacation. We recently heard about a large extended family that pools its resources and rents a large ski lodge in the Colorado mountains every year. Each of the separate families gladly simplifies its gift-giving in order to save money for the annual stay at the lodge.

A skiing Christmas works for this group on a number of different levels. Each family unit can come and go whenever it wants, there is no pressure to exchange gifts, and, best of all, there is ample opportunity for each of the thirty or so people who gather at the lodge to enjoy some physical activity. Most of the adults spend the better part of each day in cross-country skiing, while less physically active people stay behind to supervise the younger children's play in the snow. One way or another, everyone gets a much appreciated breath of fresh air.

This is such an important tradition for this family that the two grandmothers have both willed portions of their estates to provide future funds for renting the lodge.

A third thing families can do is look for lighthearted ways to add fun to their celebrations. Solemn moments have their place at Christmas, but there are also many opportunities for laughter, even silliness. For example, one family has started the tradition of passing around, year after year, the same grotesque tie. Each year, the person who received the tie the year before wraps it up and presents it to some other member of the family. The trick is to disguise it so well that no one can guess which package it's in. One year, the tie was baked in a cake; another year it was worked into the design of a wall hanging.

Finally, some people find that they can add more excitement and meaning to their holiday rituals by reaching back into the past and reviving traditions from their ethnic heritage. One woman, whose ancestors were from England, became so intrigued with the idea of a real mince pie that she learned how to make one using beef and suet. "I always used to serve mince pie," she told us, "but I would just reach for a jar on my shelf, twist off the lid, and fill a packaged pie shell. I never realized the care that went into making a real one. All the time I was chopping the meat, I was thinking that my grandmother probably did this every year for Christmas. I felt very close to her."

Sometimes finding ways to be more genuinely excited about Christmas takes some extra thought and effort. But when people value what they are doing, the added "work" becomes part of the fun of Christmas.

In the pages that follow, you will find dozens of additional suggestions for simple games, traditions, and activities to add more joy to your celebration. Most of these suggestions cost little or no money and require very little preparation time. Whether your family is large or small, intellectual or athletic, reserved or riotous, we hope you will find here at least one or two ways to have a merrier Christmas.

Exercise

FAMILY FUN

This exercise will help you clarify what kind of activities your family most enjoys and will give you some ideas for new traditions to liven up your holiday.

1. Which of the following activities are generally enjoyed by the people you celebrate Christmas with? Check those you participated in last Christmas.

- ☆ Winter sports (specify)
- ☆ Card-playing
- ☆ Game-playing
- ☆ Singing
- ☆ Playing musical instruments
- ☆ Reading aloud to each other
- ☆ Attending concerts
- ☆ Entertaining friends
- ☆ Telling anecdotes about the family
- ☆ Dancing
- ☆ Cooking together
- ☆ Going for walks
- ☆ Taking trips to the country
- ☆ Creating skits and plays
- ☆ Caroling

2. Star the activities that you would like to do this year.

By doing this exercise, many people realize that they often neglect many of their favorite activities at Christmas. Adding just one enjoyable tradition is often all it takes to have a more rewarding celebration.

Questions and Answers

Question 1: *Even though my family is all together in one physical location at Christmas, we seem to stay emotionally distant. Is there any way to bring us all closer together?*

Answer: Some families are naturally outgoing, but others need a little encouragement. First, to set the stage, check to make sure that your family celebration has neither too many activities nor too few. When there's too much going on, people often have to retreat inside themselves to find peace of mind. And when there are too few activities, people tend to become bored and seek refuge in solitary pursuits.

Second, you may want to add a family ritual through which you can express your love in a more direct way than giving gifts. In many countries, people have Christmas traditions that help them openly show their affection. In Poland, for example, families share special crackers (Oplateks) embossed with the Nativity scene before Christmas Eve dinner. When the ceremony begins, each family member is given a wafer. Then the father and mother embrace and express their love for each other, and each takes a bite from the other's Oplatek. This ritual is repeated until each person has shared his Oplatek and a few kind words with every other family member. Sharing of the Oplatek is so important to Poles that they mail crackers to relatives and close friends who are unable to join them at Christmas.

Consider beginning *your* Christmas dinner with a special ritual to remind you of why you are all together. It can be as simple as a prayer, a toast, a candle-lighting ceremony, or just a few quiet moments holding hands.

In addition, here are some more ideas to bring your family closer together: Ask family members to bring items for a "Family

Museum." Suitable things would be old photographs, diaries, heirlooms, written anecdotes, or genealogical information. Display them in a central place and people will be brought together to talk about family history.

After dinner, tell family anecdotes. Who can tell the earliest one? Who has a story no one has ever heard before? How many versions are there of the same family story? (You may want to tape this session.)

If you have home movies of your family, bring them out and play them for the assembled relatives. Everyone likes to see how people have grown and changed.

Question 2: *How can we add more excitement to our holiday food? It's not very inspired.*

Answer: You may find that simply adding more drama and ceremony to your traditional food will make it more fun for everyone. In the past, there were elaborate rituals surrounding the preparation and presentation of many holiday foods. For example, here is an account of how eggnog was made on a Southern plantation, according to a December 1889 *Ladies' Home Journal:*

> By the time our stockings were emptied and examined, grandpa, fully dressed, had come out of his room into the hall where . . . all the material for making eggnog had been set out on a gigantic scale—a fanner of fresh eggs, great dishes of sugar, and the cellaret of liquors. When the eggs were beaten to the required degree, viz., until the yolks were the color of rich cream and the whites adhered steadily to the dish when it was turned upside down, the whole was put together in the gigantic china punch-bowl, relic of ancestral feastings across seas in "ye old Countrie." I would not dare to say how many eggs, or how much brandy and rum went into the concoction of that bowl of egg nog. When it was pronounced right, a waiter of glasses was filled and handed round to the assembled company;

> and then "the stand"—a great circular, claw-footed mahogany table—was lifted out on the wide front piazza, the flaming sconces were lighted, and the egg-nog bowl, surrounded by pyramids of tumblers, was placed upon it. Then we proceeded to "drink in Christmas."

Our modern way of serving eggnog is to buy it ready-made in plastic cartons at the grocer's and serve it anytime from Thanksgiving to New Year's. If you like eggnog, consider making it from scratch on Christmas Day and drinking *your* Christmas in. You will probably find yourself serving your homemade nog with more pride and ceremony.

Be on the lookout for ways to add drama to your other holiday favorites, too. For example, if you traditionally serve plum pudding at Christmas, douse it with warm brandy, light it, turn down the dining room lights, and bring the pudding in with proper pomp and circumstance. For added interest, you may want to use this adaptation of an authentic recipe, which was judged the best of five hundred entries submitted to a London newspaper in 1876.

Proper Plum Pudding

1 pound currants
1 pound raisins
1 pound suet (Modern tastes might prefer less suet.)
¾ pound dried bread crumbs
½ nutmeg, grated (about 1 teaspoon)
¼ pound brown sugar
1 lemon rind, grated
½ pound minced, candied orange peel
5 eggs
½ pint brandy

Clean, wash, and dry the currants and raisins. Mix all the dry ingredients together. Beat the eggs, add them to the brandy, then pour over the dry ingredients and mix thoroughly. Pack into small greased kettles or molds and steam for 6 hours (makes 6 pounds). Serve with hard sauce or brandy sauce.

A final way to make your holiday food more enjoyable is to involve more people in its preparation. Set aside a leisurely afternoon, gather several friends or family members, put a Christmas record on the turntable, and make one of your favorite recipes. You may want to reenact a pioneer Christmas tradition and invite a dozen friends in for a taffy pull. There are few cooking activities that can happily involve so many people. One person can mix the ingredients. Another can monitor the candy thermometer. Two people can cut the paper to wrap the candies. Young children can butter the cooking trays. Everyone will want turns pulling the taffy. And when the taffy is done, all hands can sit around a table to shape and wrap the candy. Here is a recipe for vanilla taffy (makes two pounds), and five ways to change the flavoring.

Taffy

2½ cups sugar
1½ cups light corn syrup
1⅓ cups water
2 tablespoons vinegar
1 teaspoon salt
¼ cup butter
2 teaspoons vanilla (Omit for some of the variations.)

Have someone butter two baking pans with rims to receive the hot taffy syrup. (If you want to make chocolate taffy, grate 1 ounce of unsweetened chocolate over the bottom of the tray.) Combine all the ingredients except the butter and flavoring in a heavy 3-quart saucepan. Cook and stir over low heat until the sugar is dissolved. Turn the burner on high and cook without stirring until the candy reaches 265 degrees. Remove from the heat and add the butter. Pour carefully into buttered pans. (Make sure children are far away from the very hot syrup.) Cool until a dent remains when you press your finger into the syrup. Sprinkle on the flavoring, butter your hands or coat them with cornstarch, and gather the taffy into your hands. (Make sure it is cool enough to handle.) Pull into long ropes, double over, and pull again, until the taffy loses some of its gloss, turns lighter in color, and becomes stiffer, and ridges appear on the ropes as you stretch it out. Cut the long taffy ropes into small pieces with buttered scissors. Shape into cubes, balls, or ovals and wrap individually in waxed paper or plastic wrap. (You will want lots of help with the shaping and wrapping, for otherwise it becomes tedious.)

Other taffy flavors:
Add grated chocolate; keep vanilla
Add grated chocolate and 2 teaspoons instant coffee; keep vanilla
Add 1½ cups chopped nuts; keep vanilla
Omit vanilla; add ½ teaspoon peppermint extract
Omit vanilla; add ¼ teaspoon cinnamon oil and red food coloring

If making taffy seems too ambitious, how about roasting some chestnuts on an open fire (or in your oven if you don't have a fireplace)? To roast chestnuts, cut a cross in the flat side of the chestnut and place near (not in) the coals of an open fire until done. Stir them around once or twice to even out the heat. Or place on a cooky sheet in a 350-degree oven for twenty minutes. Take off the shells, salt, and eat as a snack, or dip in chocolate for dessert.

Finally, if you usually go to church on Christmas Eve, have a special midnight supper when you come home (called a *Reveillon* in France). A traditional French menu might include *cassoulet* (a poultry and bean casserole that can bake in the oven while you are at church), fresh French bread, cheese, a nice bottle of wine or champagne, and *bûche de Noël* (a Yule log cake that is sponge cake filled with buttercream and decorated with chocolate buttercream). You will find recipes for *cassoulet* and *bûche de Noël* in most comprehensive American cookbooks. Or make it simple. Have omelets, French bread, cheese, and red wine.

Question 3: What are some good games to play at Christmas?

Answer: Each family has its own style of game-playing. Some like deadly serious games of bridge or backgammon, while others like noisy poker games or board games such as Clue or Monopoly. But since we've observed that family Christmases could stand a good dose of levity, here are two especially silly, unserious games for you to consider. These simple card games can be played by all family members six or older.

Spoons is usually regarded as a children's game, but if adults can be encouraged to abandon their reserve, everyone should have a rousing time. To play, you will need a deck of cards and some teaspoons—one fewer than you have players. Before you begin, sort the cards into piles of like numbers. You will use as many sets of four as you have players. Set aside the remaining cards.

Deal out the cards around the circle until each player has four cards, and place the spoons in the middle of the table so that each player has quick access to a spoon. The object of the game is to get all four cards of the same number. When the game begins, the players look at their cards, choose one card each to discard, and pass the discards simultaneously to the players on their left. The players examine their new cards, choose their discards, and then on cue pass them to the left again. The first person to get four of a kind grabs (or sneaks) a spoon. As soon as one spoon is taken, anyone can grab, and the person who isn't quick enough to get one is retired from the game. (You can give the youngest children a handicap by placing spoons especially close to them.)

At the end of each hand, one player, one spoon, and one set of cards is removed from the game, until the last hand, when only two players, one spoon, and two sets of four remain. The winner is the first one to get four of a kind and grab the last spoon.

"I doubt it" is another game you may remember from your childhood, but it gains an added dimension when played by a mixture of children and conniving adults. For this game, you will need a deck of cards and three or four players, or two decks of cards and five to eight players, or three decks of cards and eight to twelve players.

Deal out all the cards. The first person to the left of the dealer begins by taking from one to four cards (one to eight if you are using two decks and one to twelve if you are using three decks) from his hand and placing them face down in the middle of the table, declaring, "Aces." The second player takes from one to four cards from his hand and places them face down in the middle of the table, saying, "Twos." The third player does the same, declaring, "Threes." Each player must play at least one card, continuing the sequence of numbers.

The object of the game is to get rid of your cards while declaring them to be the next number in sequence. Since you do not have to reveal the true identity of the cards as you lay them down, you can be either telling the truth or bluffing.

But if someone suspects that you are bluffing, he can say, "I doubt it." Then you have to turn over the cards you just put down and show their true value. If you were telling the truth and all the cards are the number you declared them to be, the person who doubted you has to put into his hand all the cards in the middle of the table. If you were bluffing, however, *you* have to pick up all the cards. The first person to lay down all his cards wins.

There are plenty of other good games. If you have very young children at your celebration, play this variation of hide the thimble. While a child is out of the room, hide a small candy cane.

When he returns, everyone should sing "Jingle Bells" (when he's getting warm) or softly (when he's cold) to lead him to the candy cane.

Then, when the children are tucked away in bed, play a game that was a great Victorian Christmas favorite: snapdragon. Here is how the game was described in the *Illustrated London News* a hundred years ago:

> The large pewter dish filled with spirit [brandy] is placed on the floor and attracts the attention of all the party. The light is applied—the flame burns beautifully azure, tipped with amber and scarlet, and whisks and frisks in a manner delightful to contemplate. . . . Throw in the plums [currants]. The spirit burns, the dish is a lake of fire; and he who can gather the prize from the jaws of perils is welcome to it. "Fortune favours the bold!" "Faint heart never won a plum!"

The object is to pluck a glowing currant and pop it into your mouth before your fingers are burned by the "snapdragon."

If your family likes to play charades, organize an elaborate charade party for the day after Christmas. In Victorian England, the charade parties on Boxing Day (December 26) were often looked forward to as much as Christmas itself.

If you're not up to charades, buy your family a new board game or a jigsaw puzzle to be opened on December 26. Then you can draw the family together and have a good way to wind down from the festivities.

Question 4: I'd like to read aloud to my family at Christmastime. What are some good reading selections?

Answer: Before the days of television, reading aloud was a favorite family pastime. Christmas is a good time to revive this custom. You might want to start with a simple Christmas story you won't find anywhere else. We discovered this pioneer letter at the Oregon Historical Society. It was written by a man named George Hines.

I am reminded of my first Christmas in Oregon, in 1853. My parents and the four of us children had just arrived in Oregon in October of that year. We had no money and only the clothes we had worn across the plains. We were loaned an old cabin to live in until we could build our own, and Father and I dug potatoes on shares for the man who owned the cabin.

All that winter we ate potatoes and boiled wheat and drank rain water.

In December, my sister and I began thinking about Christmas. I thought the prospect was pretty poor, and when we spoke to my mother, she gave us little encouragement. Dad was away working and we barely had enough to eat. All our shoes had holes.

But on Christmas Eve, Mother told us to hang up our stockings. I had no socks, but Mother made a kind of pocket to serve the purpose out of a coat, the sleeves of which I had worn to shreds. So my sister's stockings, very much darned, and my pocket were hung on pegs behind the stove, and we crept into our trundle beds.

Christmas morning came, and I built a fire in the old stove, and by the light of the pitch sticks, I discovered that there was something in our stockings. She found a doughnut doll baby, and an apple. I had an ordinary doughnut and an apple in mine.

It is doubtful that there will ever be more joy in the hearts of any children on Christmas morning.

You can also go to the library and check out one of these classics: *A Child's Christmas in Wales,* by Dylan Thomas; *Old Christmas,* by Washington Irving; *A Christmas Carol,* by Charles Dickens; "The Gift of the Magi," by O. Henry; *A Christmas Memory,* by Truman Capote. For children: *On the*

Banks of Plum Creek, by Laura Ingalls Wilder; *Little Women,* by Louisa May Alcott; "The Fir Tree," by Hans Christian Andersen; *Amahl and the Night Visitors,* by Gian-Carlo Menotti; "A Visit From St. Nicholas," by Clement Moore.

Question 5: Our family celebration seems like a blur of people and activities. How can we slow down enough to enjoy Christmas and each other?

Answer: One of the best ways to focus the group's energy is to vary the pace of the day. Try alternating physical action with more subdued activities like reading together or telling family anecdotes.

The family gift-opening can be either a frenzy of torn paper or a centered, delightful experience. If yours is a Christian family, consider beginning your present-opening by reading the Christmas story in Luke. Then open the presents one at a time and take time to appreciate each one. Show young children photographs of faraway relatives who sent them gifts and say a little about them.

Finally, even if you don't normally go to church, you may find that attending a Christmas service will add peace and harmony to your family celebration.

Question 6: I enjoy Christmas music, but all we do is listen to it. How can I get my family more interested in singing?

Answer: Although they may not always admit it, most people like to sing. Often all it takes is one brave soul to get things going. Gather around the piano or sing your favorite carols a cappella. Add to the general merriment by trying to harmonize.

How about going caroling? In early American history caroling was often a rowdy affair where people would band together and go from home to home banging on pots and pans, trying to get all the neighbors to come along. Then they would sing (and drink) until early in the morning. While we can't recommend this particular variation, you may want to make your caroling more lively by trying to entice your neighbors into joining you, bringing along simple musical instruments, or carrying candles mounted on poles.

***Question** 7: I've always wanted a real Yule log. How do you do it?*

Answer: To carry out this ritual as it used to be done, you need a large, open fireplace and easy access to the woods. First, gather up a special Yule-log search party, and then comb the woods for a large, knotty, water-soaked hardwood log. On Christmas morning, make a hot fire with dry kindling and smaller pieces of wood, and top it with the Yule log. As long as the Yule log burns (and you may be able to keep it burning for several days), follow the ancient tradition and ban all nonessential work. When the log finally burns out, save a piece of it to start next year's Yule log.

***Question** 8: When we've opened our gifts, Christmas is as good as done with. What are some ways to keep Christmas alive for the rest of the holiday season?*

Answer: Children, especially, need some way to occupy themselves when the gift-exchange is over. After opening your gifts, how about giving a Christmas treat to the birds? Decorate a tree close to your living room window with bird food so the whole family can enjoy watching them feed. If you put out a variety of food, you'll attract more than one kind of bird. Here are some recommendations:

☆ Unsalted peanuts in shells, strung with heavy-duty thread
☆ Apple pieces

- ☆ Beef suet
- ☆ Bread crumbs dipped in peanut butter
- ☆ Breadsticks
- ☆ Rice cakes
- ☆ Popcorn

If your children are at all theatrical, ask them to prepare a skit or play to give the day after Christmas. You can check books out of the library with simple Christmas plays, or let them dream up a simple plot of their own. Encourage them to dress up and add songs.

When the holiday season draws to a close, you might want to have an end-of-Christmas ceremony. Gather the family together to take the ornaments off the tree and carefully pack them away. If you have a live tree, replant it outdoors or put it in a sheltered place until the ground thaws. If you have a cut tree, either burn it (carefully) or decorate it with food for the birds. One family explained to us that making a special occasion of ending the holiday "put a seal on Christmas, and promised that it would come again."

☆

Appendix:
Resources for a Simple Christmas

Over the years, many people have asked us for specific advice on how to make Christmas simpler. After they have decided that they want their celebrations to be easier, more value centered, more personal, and less expensive, they often become interested in specific suggestions. In this section of the book, you will find the best ideas we have run across for simplifying Christmas and making it more enjoyable at the same time. Many of these suggestions come from the people we have interviewed and people who have come to our workshops. Others were inspired by current books and magazines, or accounts of past Christmases. And still others have been adapted from our own personal observations and experiences.

Most of them center on simplifying holiday preparations and gift-giving, since these are the two parts of Christmas that tend to get most overblown and complicated. We suggest that you read over the ideas in each category that interest you and choose one or two to try next Christmas. Some of the ideas will help you save money or time, some will help you feel more personally involved in Christmas, and others will help you find added depth and meaning in your celebration. Whether you decide to adopt any of these suggestions exactly as presented or use them to inspire your own creative thoughts, we hope you will gain a new appreciation for the simple joys of Christmas.

DECORATIONS

Bringing down the boxes of ornaments from the attic, polishing the candlesticks, replacing the burned-out tree lights, and sorting the greens and ribbon for the front door wreath—all of these decorating activities are integral parts of Christmas for most people. Through their own natural beauty and intimate association with happy times, a lighted tree, candles, and all the other beloved objects of the season can transform your everyday surroundings into something magical. No matter how many other things people may want to change about the holiday, very few would eliminate Christmas decorations entirely.

But lots of people would welcome a reduction in the amount of time, effort, and money they spend decorating for the holidays. They want to be able to delight in the physical beauty of Christmas without being preoccupied with the way Christmas looks. On the following pages, you will find simple decorating suggestions that will provide the setting for a wonderful Christmas without overtaxing your energy or pocketbook.

GREENS

"It is pleasant to awake on Christmas morning in familiar surroundings, yet made unfamiliar by a green Yuletide welcome."

—HOUSE BEAUTIFUL, 1911

Bringing in greens is a wonderful way to transform your everyday environment into a festive one. Even if you do nothing more than highlight them with an occasional red ribbon or colorful ornament, their appearance is enough to announce that it is Christmas. But besides their beauty, they have other advantages: (1) you can often gather them yourself for nothing, or purchase them at garden shops inexpensively; (2) they have a long and honorable association with Christmas; and (3) you don't have to be an artist to make them look good.

Man-made ornaments didn't become generally available in the United States until the 1870s, so greens were about the only decorations there were. Here are some nineteenth-century ideas to inspire you:

☆ Arrange a combination of ferns, evergreens, and holly berries in a vase, instead of flowers, and use as a table centerpiece.
☆ Place a small stem of holly on each cloth dinner napkin on Christmas Day.
☆ Use holly to decorate your wrapped packages. The plainer the wrapping paper, the better.
☆ Outline doorways, moldings, architectural details and picture frames with evergreen garlands. (This was the classic nineteenth-century treatment.)
☆ Collect dried flowers, weeds, cones, leaves, and corn husks for use in wreaths or table arrangements. Suggestions: goldenrod and milkweed pods dry without special preserving; thistles, leaves, and berries can be preserved by sticking the stems in a solution of one part glycerin (from a drugstore) to two parts water; flowers, such as Queen Anne's lace, can be placed in airtight boxes and surrounded with silica gel until they are completely dried and quite brittle; cones can be left natural, cut in half to reveal their beautiful patterns, glittered, or painted gold and used as accents in wreaths and other arrangements.
☆ If you live in a mild climate, bring in branches of forsythia, cherry, or other flowering trees and force-bloom them in

time for Christmas. It was the custom in many European countries to bring the branches inside on St. Barbara's Day, December 4, and try to get them to bloom for Christmas Eve. Any unmarried girl who accomplished this was sure to find a husband before the New Year was out.

☆ Decorate any indoor plant or tree that has branches with small ornaments. Small red ribbons on a Norfolk Island pine, masses of white lights on a large jade tree, and a ficus festooned with colorful popcorn and cranberry strings are examples. In addition, dried flower blossoms, nuts (plain or gilded), and raffia ornaments are colorful and light enough for indoor plants.

Although it's fun to look around your house and think of ways to decorate with plants you already have, there is a special pleasure in using traditional greens. Here's a little history on each one.

Mistletoe was a sacred plant with magical properties for ancient European peoples, long before its more playful association with Christmas. In medieval Europe, *holly* and *ivy* were the most important Christmas greens. In the old carol "The Holly and the Ivy" holly represents men and ivy represents women as they argue in fun over which sex is superior. *Rosemary* was prized at Christmas for its pungent scent and its long-lasting leaves. In the Scandinavian countries, *wheat sheaves* were saved from the harvest and mounted on tall poles for good luck during the coming year. In Eastern European countries, *straw* was also placed on tables or on the floor as a reminder of the stable where Jesus was born. *Poinsettias,* now a common Christmas motif, were cultivated by the Aztecs in Mexico, and first incorporated into the Christmas celebration by the Franciscan monks in Mexico in the seventeenth century.

CANDLES

"If there is a mantel and it is filled with things—off must come the things. When it is as bare as Mother Hubbard's cupboard, bring out all the candlesticks in the house for inspection."

—HOUSE BEAUTIFUL, 1908

In addition to greens, candles are a simple and natural way to decorate for Christmas, and if you shop wisely or make your own, they can also be inexpensive. Candles have always been an important part of the winter festival, even predating the Christian celebration itself. In Europe, the lighting of the Christmas Eve candle by the oldest member of the household has been an important ritual for centuries. In Sweden, candles were indispensable to the Lucia Festival, in which the oldest daughter in each family was dressed in white and crowned with a circle of lighted tapers. In the late Middle Ages, pyramids made of tiers of wooden shelves were decorated with candles and carried in processions. In Mexico, candles were put in brown paper bags weighted with sand, and these *luminarias* were used to light the paths of Christmas processions. The Jewish celebration of Hanukkah centers on the ritual of lighting, on successive nights, eight candles held in a candelabrum called a *menorah.* And many Christian families today celebrate Advent by the ceremonious lighting of candles in a special Advent wreath.

But aside from these ritual uses, candles are part of Christmas because people like them. Nothing can make our world into a softer, more beautiful place faster than candles. Recently we visited a home where the only Christmas decorations were masses of candles in different parts of the main room. The electric lights were turned off, and everywhere there was a soft glow. On the mantel were groups of six or seven red votive candles in punch glasses, on the coffee table were several floating candles in glass containers, every windowsill was lit with long bayberry tapers in brass and silver candlesticks, and the buffet table was crowned with a cranberry candle surrounded by a circle of cedar boughs. It was simple and stunning. The hostess told us it was also practical. Candles offer variety, they smell delicious, they are traditional, and the light is so flattering that you can relax about vacuuming and dusting.

When you think about candles, experiment with holders. Some possibilities: wineglasses; cake and muffin tins; trivets; egg-cups; soap dishes; clay or plastic plant pots filled with sand, dirt, or gravel. Add small inexpensive mirrors to reflect more light. A glass hurricane-lamp globe can be placed over a candle for a special effect. (And don't forget kerosene lamps themselves. They can be as expensive or inexpensive as you wish, and if you have the kind with a clear glass reservoir, colored lamp oil will brighten your room.)

AROMATIC DECORATIONS

For many people, nothing is as pleasant or memorable at Christmas as the way it smells. And often what smells good is also beautiful to look at. Here are some simple things to make:

☆ Pomander balls: Stud a thick-skinned orange with cloves (about one pound of cloves for a dozen oranges). After they have drained for a day on paper towels, roll them in ground spices, such as cinnamon, ginger, allspice. If you also add ground orris root to this mixture, it will act as a fixative and preserve the fragrance longer. You can then use a big needle threaded with ribbon or string to hang the balls, or wrap them with colorful ribbon, or pile them high in decorative bowls and use them in plant arrangements.

☆ Potpourri: Collect broken pieces of herbs, spices, and flowers in pretty glass containers, and decorate with ribbon, yarn, or small ornaments. Some common garden ingredients are mint, rosemary, roses, thyme, lilac, and lavender. You can also add dried citrus peel and cinnamon sticks. Be sure all the ingredients are absolutely dry to prevent mold, and collect three or four times the amount you want to have when everything has dried and settled. If you keep a lid on the container and only open it occasionally, the fragrance will last longer.

☆ Fresh Fruit: Of course, there are strings of cranberries, but don't forget other winter fruits that can add both aroma and color to Christmas. Red apples can be piled high in baskets or stacked in pyramids in shallow glass containers. Several fresh fruits can be grouped on evergreens, and spread along a mantel or side table and accented with nuts. Citrus fruits, pineapples, apples, and pears are especially suitable.

☆ Simple Smells: In addition, it is easy to arrange cinnamon sticks in shallow trays, or burn incense and pungent candles. And nothing is quite as wonderful as the smell of burning wood if yours is among the eighteen million American households that have fireplaces, or the six million that own wood stoves.

THE TREE

Although greens and candles and pomander balls can add grace and beauty to your decorating, it's the tree that takes center stage at Christmas. For many people, Christmas *is* the tree, even though it is a relative newcomer to the celebration. It wasn't until Queen Victoria's German husband, Prince Albert, decorated a tree for the royal family in 1848 that the custom caught on in England and America. Now most people can't imagine Christmas without one.

Perhaps the easiest and simplest kind of Christmas tree to have is an artificial one with ornaments permanently attached. This is a boon to many of the older people we have talked to, who find going out and getting a freshly cut evergreen and dragging it back to their apartments more than they can manage. And it may also be the answer for people who live in urban areas where evergreens are in short supply or are quite expensive.

But for many people, a real tree captures best all the good feelings they have about Christmas. Certainly a beautifully conceived and decorated tree is a pleasure, and books and magazines are filled to overflowing with ideas on how to decorate one with ingenuity and taste. But the way a tree looks is only part (if a very important part) of how people feel about it. Most people also respond to the sentimental value of familiar ornaments, whether they are beautiful or not. And they tend to get more enjoyment from the tree if they have had a good time decorating it. A tree decorated by one person spending a lot of time will often have a gratifying artistic unity to it, but a tree that involves the whole family is often more satisfying overall.

It's fun to make the tree a special family tradition, with each person playing an important part. Here are some suggestions for a "family tree":

☆ Assign everyone a task. Many men enjoy taking their kids out to get the tree, but they're not always involved in decorating it. Ask yourself what special job could be done by each family member. Certain ornaments could be reserved for each child to hang; the crowning star or angel could be the privilege of the littlest child, held up by the father. Sometimes, it might make sense to leave the entire decorating to the children and/or the father.

☆ Make getting and decorating the tree a ritual:

Set aside a whole day if possible, which everyone in the family reserves in advance.

If you live near a tree farm, take the children and cut your own. When you get home, warm yourself with hot chocolate before the fire.

Have a tree-trimming party for the neighbors or your extended family. In advance, get the tree settled in the stand, strings of lights in good working order, some unbreakable ornaments for little ones to put on, simple materials for making ornaments if you wish, and good things to eat and drink.

While your family decorates the tree, put your favorite Christmas music on the stereo, serve eggnog, and light the fire and the candles (but not on the tree, of course—candles on a tree are a fire hazard).

☆ Have every member of your family contribute ornaments to the tree. Encourage them to think of found objects or things that are simple to make: paper clip chains, costume jewelry, rickrack, cookie cutters hung with ribbons, small baskets, paper flowers, tinfoil balls, small toys, and wood shavings.

Many families get great satisfaction from having a living tree that is brought inside from year to year, or purchased new every year and then replanted outside. It can be decorated inexpensively and naturally with tangerines, apples, walnuts, dried grasses and flowers, cones, berries, cranberries, and popcorn. You can replant it by digging a hole one and a half times larger than the root mass, lowering it into the hole, loosening (but not removing) the burlap bag that surrounds it, filling the hole with dirt, surrounding the tree with straw or some other kind of mulch, and watering well. If you live in a part of the country that gets frost until spring, you will want to dig your hole in November before the ground freezes. When you think about living trees, don't forget that outside trees can be decorated for the animals with strings of popcorn, rice cakes, hard rolls, wild bird seed, and nuts.

Many of the families we have talked to like to decorate their trees with ornaments that symbolize important family events. If you are interested in this kind of "family history tree," you can do the following:

☆ Give your child, or grandchild, an ornament every Christmas. When the child grows up and celebrates her first Christmas away from home, surprise her by sending a box filled with her own ornaments early in December.

☆ Collect ornaments (or souvenirs that could become ornaments) on your year-round family excursions. When they are all hanging up on the Christmas tree, you will have visual reminders of your travels together.

☆ Encourage your young child to make things to hang on the tree. Even though some contributions (colored paper, ribbons, drawings, cut paper) are only used once, save and label them to show to your child when he or she is grown.

☆ Choose an ornament each year that represents an important family event—a new baby, a new house, a graduation, a new job.

MUSIC

Brightening your physical environment is one way to change an everyday mood into a festive one, but perhaps nothing can lift your spirits faster than music. All you have to do is hear your favorite Christmas composition or carol, and you are transported back through pleasant memories of the past and filled with the joy and hope of the coming celebration. Even if the tree, the presents, and the big turkey dinner were all taken away, it would still be Christmas—if you had Christmas music.

Owning your own albums is wonderful, but you don't have to be limited by the amount of money you have to spend on them. Most local libraries have a wide selection of Christmas records to choose from, and taking potluck can be an adventure. You never know when you might stumble across a record that will add something new to your enjoyment of the holiday. But if you want guidance, here are some suggestions:

☆ *Christmas from Clare* (Argo) with John Rutter conducting the musicians of Clare College, Cambridge, England, contains some familiar carols ("I Saw Three Ships") and some unfamiliar ones ("Donkey Carol" and "Cradle Song").
☆ The 1981 recording of *Messiah* (Smithsonian Collection, three records) with James Weaver conducting the Smithsonian Chamber Players will give you a chance to hear a period rendition of Handel's classic oratorio. It is available by mail from Smithsonian Recordings, P.O. Box 10230, Des Moines, IA 50336.
☆ *A Festival of Carols in Brass* (CBS) with the Philadelphia Brass Ensemble features many familiar carols, such as "The First Noel" and "Hark! The Herald Angels Sing."
☆ *To Drive the Cold Winter Away* (Vanguard) is a spirited collection of carols and festival dances from the twelfth to eighteenth centuries, with John Sothcott directing the St. George's Canzona.
☆ *The Shepherd's Pipe: Songs for the Holy Night* (Plough Publishing House, Society of Brothers, Rifton, NY 12471) is a recording of music composed by Marilyn Swinger, a member of the Society of Brothers. She has set to music poems by an unknown poet, which were found in Germany in 1935. A 112-page book of poems, musical scores, and suggestions for a pageant is available to accompany the record.

But there are other ways to fill your celebration with music besides listening to records. You can make your own music. Regardless of how you sound, singing and playing yourself can give you satisfaction that is hard to surpass.

Caroling is the musical tradition that everyone thinks of first at Christmas. Which of us doesn't have memories of standing outside in the frosty air, raising his voice with others in glorious, out-of-tune song? But aside from providing pleasant memories, caroling has several other advantages:

☆ People of different ages can enjoy something together, especially if you carol in nursing homes and if your group is composed of both young and old people.
☆ Caroling reinforces neighborhood unity by giving you a chance to do something nice for neighbors you would not normally see.
☆ It gets people outside and physically active.
☆ It provides an important link to the outside for people who are isolated because of age or ill health.
☆ It doesn't cost anything.

If you would like to go caroling, there are a few things you can do to make it more enjoyable: (1) notify ahead of time the people or institutions (especially nursing homes) you would like to sing for; (2) make sure your singers have copies of the words to more obscure second or third verses; (3) make sure that everyone is dressed warmly enough; (4) have hot drinks available along the way or when you get back home.

But you don't have to leave your house to make your own Christmas music. Many people have told us that getting together to pound the piano and warm up on the guitar is one of the activities they enjoy most at Christmastime. How you sound seems to matter less than the spirit of fun that permeates the music. And, as one professional choir director told us, this is a good way to combat the tendency people have to be spectators at their own celebrations.

Making music at home is also an important way for children to grasp the meaning of the entire Christmas season. Several families we have talked to mark each of the four parts of the holiday—before Christmas, Christmas Eve, Christmas morning, and Epiphany when the Three Kings traveled to Bethlehem to pay homage to the Baby Jesus—with special carols. For example, "Deck the Halls," "Jingle Bells," and "O Come, O Come, Emanuel" can be sung before Christmas; "Silent Night" and "O Little Town of Bethlehem" on Christmas Eve; "Joy to the World" and "Hark! The Herald Angels Sing" on Christmas Day; and "The Twelve Days of Christmas" and "We Three Kings" during Epiphany.

If you want to play or sing Christmas music at home, here are two good resources: *The Oxford Book of Carols* edited by Percy Dearmer (Oxford: Oxford University Press, 1964) is complete and has creative settings for traditional and nontraditional carols; *The International Book of Christmas Carols* by Walter Ehret and George K. Evans (Brattleboro, Vt.: Stephen Greene Press, 1980) has a wide selection of music, with simple piano arrangements.

CHRISTMAS CARDS

Christmas cards have been a staple of the celebration for over a hundred years, and many people value them as a good way to stay in touch with those who might otherwise fade from view. But more and more people are questioning the time and expense they require and challenging the unwritten assumption that Christmas wouldn't be Christmas without them.

Ironically, Christmas cards were originally designed to save people work at Christmas. In 1843 Sir Henry Cole commissioned John Calcott Horsley to design a card that would take away the stress of having to write personal letters to all his friends and relatives at Christmas. Cards soon became so successful in England that, as soon as the postal system grew advanced enough to handle the avalanche, everyone started sending them.

Christmas cards caught on in the United States when Louis

Prang, a German immigrant lithographer, held an open competition for card artists in 1880 and began producing beautiful cards in great numbers. By the end of the 1880s, Christmas cards were lavish, and sales were in the millions.

In fact, Christmas cards were such an established part of Christmas by the late 1880s that they became a solution to the ever present gift-giving problem. It was considered just as personal to express your feelings for friends through cards as gifts—and it was a lot easier. But cards didn't replace gifts for long. Soon they were being sent *in addition* to gifts, and now many people are trying to find ways to simplify both.

Although lots of people have eliminated Christmas cards altogether, many others are uncomfortable with this abrupt ending of a once valued tradition. So they are finding ways to modify their every-friend-gets-one-card approach by making some modifications:

☆ Send your cards after Christmas, and make them seasonal cards, rather than Christmas cards. Or send them on Valentine's Day, which is less hectic for you and gives your recipients more time to enjoy them.

☆ Reduce the number of cards you must purchase, sign, address, and mail by sending them only to people you seldom see.

☆ Send birthday cards with personal notes in them to people you care about, rather than Christmas cards. While many people expect Christmas cards, they are surprised and delighted when their birthdays are remembered.

☆ To cut the cost and make your cards more personal, create simple cards by copying one of your children's drawings on a copier. They can also include a seasonal message written by your child.

☆ Instead of sending Christmas cards, write a Christmas letter. This is an easy way for you to share information about your family and saves you from having to write the same letter to several different people. Other members of your family can contribute to the writing or illustrating.

To make your Christmas cards more meaningful, you can buy them from a nonprofit corporation that supports a cause you believe in. Examples: UNICEF (see under Gift Catalogs), the National Wildlife Federation (8925 Leesburg Pike, Vienna, VA 22180), the Fellowship for Reconciliation, an international peace organization (Box 271, Nyack, NY 10960), or your local art museum.

Another way to add meaning to your cards is to buy them from local artists. Art museums, specialty shops, art schools, and galleries are good places to find them.

ENTERTAINING

The desire to get together with friends at Christmas is almost universal. We have talked to a few people who confessed they would enjoy a solitary Christmas, but most people envision a celebration filled with friends. They want to share their Christmas pleasures with those whose company they enjoy and feel comfortable in. A women's magazine recently polled its readers and found that they entertain an average of four to nine times during the holiday season. That means that a lot of people are giving thought to hosting dinners, parties, and luncheons.

It also means that a lot of people are trying to entertain on top of already full lives. How can you get together with your friends easily and simply at Christmas, and still get the feelings of fulfillment and closeness to others you want?

One of the most important things you can do for yourself is take the pressure off your own performance. Here are some suggestions to help you shift the emphasis off your skill as a cook, and simply have a good time together:

☆ Involve your guests in the preparations of the meal. For example, you could have a "Christmas leftover party," where guests bring leftover stuffing, salad, pie, and so on. Use your imagination to combine these ingredients in new ways. This gives you a chance to try other people's Christmas specialties, and makes the whole group responsible for the results.

☆ Plan a meal that your guests make themselves, such as make-your-own pizza, sandwiches, tacos, or a salad bar; or divide up the meal so the men make the lasagna and the women make the salad.

☆ Make the process of eating a ritual. Main dishes that lend themselves to ritual are cheese fondue; meat fondue, with chunks of meat fried in hot oil or stock and dipped into a variety of sauces; sausages roasted over the fire; cooked crab, to be cracked and dipped into sauce or melted butter.

☆ Plan a tasting party, in which guests provide wine, coffee, cheeses, or other food to share. Here the emphasis is on the variety and quality of the items contributed, and not on your culinary skills, although you might want to provide breads, crackers, or cookies.

☆ Organize a progressive dinner, in which each course is provided by a different household and the entire party moves from one place to another. This works especially well when everyone lives in the same neighborhood or apartment building.

☆ Issue spontaneous invitations so that no one expects a grand performance. A recent study found that the main reason women don't invite their friends to their homes more often is that they are afraid their houses aren't clean enough. As an experiment, you might invite friends over when your house is still a little rough around the edges, just to see what it feels like. If you include children in the invitation, you will change expectations in the direction of a more fun, chaotic, "happy madhouse" atmosphere.

☆ Balance the eating part of the evening with activities that encourage everyone's involvement. See the Christmas Revival chapter for suggestions for games and so forth.

In addition to taking the spotlight off your own performance, you can plan to entertain when you are less busy by having an after-Christmas party, like an Epiphany party on January 6 or an end-of-winter party in February, when your invitation will come as a welcome break rather than another social obligation to be crowded into an already busy Christmas season.

But whenever you decide to entertain, invite your guests to simpler meals. Instead of having a full-blown sit-down dinner with your best china, consider inviting your friends for brunch, for drinks, for dessert, or even for tea. If you shift the focus slightly away from the food and toward the interaction of the people present, the responsibility for a good time is shared by everyone.

Another way to make entertaining easier, though not cheaper, is to hire help. There are caterers who will prepare and serve the food and clean up afterward. There are people who will clean your house, renew your upholstery, bleach your drapes, rejuvenate your yard, remodel your bathroom, paint your smudgy walls, and deliver your flowers.

FOOD

It has always been one of the privileges of the Christmas season—a duty, almost—to eat and drink as much as possible. But even if food is an important part of your Christmas, you may have good reasons for wanting to make your food preparation easier. You may be a woman employed outside the home, or a single parent, or tired of starving yourself in January to pay for the sins of December. Or you may simply believe in an ethic of moderation. Here are some suggestions for holiday food that tastes great but will get you out of the kitchen faster.

Use one basic cookie recipe but vary it in simple ways to make different kinds of cookies. For example, vanilla refrigerator cookies can be made into butterscotch cookies or chocolate cookies by easy substitutions. And they can be transformed still further, into dropped or filled cookies.

Basic Vanilla Refrigerator Cookies

¾ cup butter
1 cup sugar
1 beaten egg
1 teaspoon vanilla
2 cups flour
½ teaspoon salt
1½ teaspoons baking powder

Beat the butter until soft, add the sugar, and mix. Add the egg and the vanilla. Stir in the flour, salt, and baking powder. Form into a 2-inch roll, place on foil, and refrigerate. After 12 hours, bake in a 400-degree oven for 8 to 10 minutes.

Variations: For butterscotch cookies, substitute brown sugar for white sugar; add coconut and/or cinnamon. For chocolate cookies, add 3 ounces of chocolate, melted and cooled, to the dough and ½ cup of chopped walnuts.

You can make all three versions, freeze the dough, and bake the cookies straight from the freezer as needed. In addition, you can vary the shapes; dust some with sugar before baking; use ¼ cup less flour to make dropped cookies; or spread layers with a fruit filling (like apricot jam) for a filled sandwich cookie.

The same principle works for fruit breads. Find one basic recipe you like and add whatever fruit or vegetable you have on hand. Here is one we especially like:

Basic Fruit Bread

⅓ cup shortening
⅔ cup sugar
1 teaspoon grated lemon rind
1 to 1½ cups fruit pulp
2 beaten eggs
1¾ cups flour
2¼ teaspoons baking powder
½ teaspoon salt

Blend the shortening, sugar, and lemon rind. Add the fruit pulp and eggs. Mix in the flour, baking powder, and salt. Bake in a greased loaf pan for 1 hour in a 350-degree oven. Note: You may have to slightly increase the amount of flour for very moist fruit pulp.

Variations: Use cinnamon, orange rind, or rum flavoring in place of lemon. Add ½ cup of nuts, or ¼ cup of dried fruit, such as apricot, or ½ cup of coconut. Fruits and vegetables we have used include banana, applesauce, cranberries, pumpkin, zucchini.

Your cookies can take on a vast array of sizes and shapes when you invite your baking friends to a "cookie-exchange party." Everyone brings six dozen cookies made with her favorite recipe. They are displayed on a big table and each person chooses the six dozen cookies of her choice. You go with one kind and come home with six different kinds. Here are some quick and delicious cookies you might bring to such a party:

Meringues

2 egg whites
1 pinch cream of tartar
½ cup sugar

Beat the egg whites and the cream of tartar until foamy. Gradually add the sugar until the mixture holds stiff peaks. Drop by the tablespoon onto a well-greased cookie sheet and bake at 225 degrees for 50 minutes.

Variations: Add ½ cup of coconut and 1 teaspoon of vanilla for coconut macaroons; add 3 tablespoons of cocoa for chocolate macaroons; or add ½ cup of ground nuts. Experiment with spices such as cinnamon and nutmeg.

But cookies don't always need to be made from scratch. Here are some ways to make good cookies fast:

☆ Buy slice-and-bake cookies and decorate them yourself with walnut halves, candied orange peel, miniature marshmallows, raisins, jams, or your own designs made with tubes of prepared frosting.

☆ For easy gingerbread men, add just enough coffee or rum to gingerbread mix to moisten it (the batter should be very stiff). Form it into a ball, roll the ball out on a generously floured board, and cut it into shapes with a gingerbread cookie cutter. Bake at 350 degrees for ten to twelve minutes.

☆ For easy bar cookies, use a cookie mix and follow the directions on the box for bar cookie variations. To make them festive, add mincemeat, candied fruit, or nuts.

☆ If you find yourself too rushed to make dinner some December evening, consider having a "dipping-into-the-pot" dinner. The idea originated with the Swedish custom of *doppa y grytan.* In Sweden families gather around the pot, where the Christmas ham or sausage has been simmering for many hours, and dip pieces of heavy rye bread into the broth for a light meal or a prelude to a more sumptuous one. If you don't happen to have a ham or sausage simmering, you can use canned or homemade beef or chicken broth. Augment the meal with hunks of cheese, fruit, and wine.

Don't be afraid to use prepared ingredients in your holiday food. For example:

☆ Simple marinated vegetables can be made by adding fresh mushrooms and canned pimentos to purchased marinated artichoke hearts. The marinade from the artichokes will be sufficient for all the vegetables.

☆ For simple hors d'oeuvres, unwrap a block of cream cheese, pour a few tablespoons of soy sauce over it, and surround with crackers.

☆ Canned creamed herring can be purchased in the meat department of your grocery store. Serve it with crackers, canned pickled beets, and dill pickles.

☆ Don't forget popcorn. Try it flavored with pepper and Parmesan cheese, or drizzled with garlic butter and herbs.

☆ To serve a delicious sauerkraut side dish, rinse the sauerkraut under running tap water and squeeze out all the moisture. Then sauté it in butter with sliced onions, white or red wine, and caraway seeds.

More ideas for desserts and food preparation:

☆ For an elegant and different dessert that can be made in minutes, try this recipe:

Almond Cake

1 cube butter (½ cup)
½ cup sugar
1 cup canned almond paste (found in the gourmet section of most grocery stores)
3 eggs
2 tablespoons flour
¼ teaspoon salt
1 teaspoon vanilla
¼ teaspoon almond extract
powdered sugar

Cream the butter and sugar together. Add the almond paste and mix well. Add the eggs and beat. Mix in the flour, salt, and flavorings. Pour into an 8-inch cake pan and bake for 45 minutes at 350 degrees. The cake will be moist. If you want it to look festive, cut a snowflake pattern from a piece of light cardboard, place it over the top of the cooled cake, and sift powdered sugar lightly over it. The sugar will fall into the holes in your design, and when you lift off the paper, the cake will be decorated with a snowflake design in sugar. Refrigerate and serve chilled.

☆ For another easy dessert, prepared mincemeat mixed with a little brandy or rum (if you have it) is delicious over vanilla ice cream.

☆ Many people are finding ways to simplify Christmas Eve dinner, in anticipation of the abundant delights of the next day, by serving soup with fresh bread and fruit. For an easy soup, try this:

Curried Pumpkin Soup

⅓ cup chopped green onions
3 tablespoons butter or margarine
2½ cups canned chicken broth
2 cups canned pumpkin
salt and pepper to taste
2 teaspoons lemon juice
1 teaspoon curry powder
nutmeg

Sauté the onion in the butter until tender. Add the rest of the ingredients (except the nutmeg) and simmer for 10 minutes. Sprinkle with the nutmeg and serve.

☆ Restrict your Christmas baking to the week before Christmas to keep your time in the kitchen and the amount you eat under control. An added benefit is that you won't get tired of Christmas specialties.

☆ Many people discover that some part of their holiday food preparations falls into the "excessive" category. Consider making half the number of cookies you usually bake, or eliminating the third pie at Christmas dinner.

☆ By accepting the sometimes less-than-perfect results of your children's cooking and welcoming the participation of your husband, you can spend less time in the kitchen doing less complicated dishes. Establish food traditions that depend on the involvement of every family member. Find out what your husband and children would like to make, and make it—year after year.

☆ Your children may be able to do more to help you than you think. Consider asking children six to ten years old to help in the following ways:

Making place cards for the dinner table
Setting the table
Measuring baking ingredients and pouring them into the mixer
Simple chopping, peeling, slicing, and grating
Icing and decorating cookies
Running errands
Answering the phone and taking messages
Forming cookies on a cookie sheet
Washing dishes and cleaning up

☆ Even if you can't afford caterers who cook, serve, and clean up after special parties, you may find that buying baked goods or buffet meats and cheeses from a delicatessen is worth the extra expense.

☆ Do you know of a lonely friend or neighbor, perhaps a grandmother, who would welcome the hustle and bustle of your kitchen for a little while? She can help you make cookies then take some home for herself.

HEALTHY FOOD

In addition to wanting to make Christmas food preparation easier, you may also want it to be healthier. Many people monitor their children's sugar intake and carefully watch their own calories all year—except at Christmas.

"Every year I engage in this gargantuan battle between Thanksgiving and New Year's. Here I am in the middle of this diet, and along comes Christmas. And the fudge. And I eat too much, and am defeated once again."

While most people will want to indulge in extra calories sometime during the season, they also want to be able to enjoy Christmas without getting out of control. Here are some nutritious and festive ideas.

When you are giving food gifts, consider:

- ☆ Homemade French, rye, or whole wheat bread
- ☆ Homemade crackers
- ☆ A basket filled with nuts and a nutcracker
- ☆ Home-canned pickles, relishes, and chutneys
- ☆ Fancy or unusual cheeses
- ☆ Fine wines
- ☆ Frozen berries you picked yourself the previous summer (if you were provident enough to plan ahead)
- ☆ Dried fruits instead of candied fruits in fruit breads
- ☆ Selected teas and coffees
- ☆ Your own special salad dressing
- ☆ Sourdough starter for bread
- ☆ Homemade pasta noodles
- ☆ Home-canned mincemeat or pumpkin pie filling
- ☆ Gourmet specialties, such as imported mustard, rice wine

vinegar, soy sauce, capers, green peppercorns, smoked fish, etc.

When you are planning holiday food for your own children, consider:

☆ Hot cider with cinnamon sticks
☆ Bowls of popcorn, pretzels, and peanuts for snacks
☆ Meals that focus attention on the main course and take the pressure off dessert, like cheese fondue; hot dogs roasted on sticks in the fireplace; pizzas on two-foot-long hero sandwiches the kids put together themselves
☆ Small treats of sugarless candy
☆ Fresh and dried fruit after dinner
☆ Baked apples for dessert
☆ Party mixes, such as the following:

PARTY MIX

¾ cup butter
1½ teaspoons salt
5 teaspoons Worcestershire sauce
8 cups rice, corn, and wheat cereals in any combination
1 cup pretzels
1 cup salted peanuts

Coat the mixture with melted butter and bake in a shallow baking pan at 250 degrees for about an hour. Stir occasionally.

GIFTS

Of all our modern Christmas traditions, gift-giving seems to take the most time, money, and energy. It's not uncommon for people to spend hundreds of dollars and weeks of effort on this one part of Christmas alone. Although few people want to banish gifts altogether, most of them are looking for ways to make the ritual more enjoyable and less of a strain. In the pages that follow, you will find money-saving gift ideas, time-saving gift ideas, alternative gift ideas, and alternative gift sources.

SAVING MONEY

Making your own gifts, of course, can save you a lot of money. If you have the time, talent, and energy to devote to a homemade Christmas, there are many wonderful resources to choose from.

However, like many of the people we talk to, you may have as little extra time as money. But even if you buy most of your gifts, there are still ways to cut down on the expense:

- ☆ If you take a predetermined amount of money out of the bank before you go shopping and declare your credit cards and checks off limits, you will not only save on the high cost of credit, but you will probably make better spending decisions.
- ☆ Be on the lookout for special sales. For example, stores are fiercely competitive with their name-brand toys, so be sure to do some comparison shopping. You may find the same toy for 25 percent less at another store. And if you're shopping for small home appliances, look for rebates. There are many more of them in December than the rest of the year.
- ☆ If you want to save money on gifts, you don't have to look further than your favorite cookbook. The traditional candies, cookies, and fruit bread are always appreciated, but consider making pasta, pesto, herb vinegars, herb bouquets, rye bread, chutney, champagne jelly, citron, smoked fish, cheese balls, snack mixes, your own Tom and Jerry mix, cranberry bread, nut bread, tea blends, coffee blends, your own mustard.

Tempt fate. Buy your gifts and tree right before Christmas to take advantage of last-minute price-slashing.

☆ Buy inexpensive gifts and let your presentation turn them into elegant ones. For example, to dress up your food gifts, buy a simple basket with an open weave and thread red ribbon through the holes. Wrap the goodies in colored cellophane, arrange them artfully in the basket, and add a handsome card. This way, a dozen cookies can be transformed into a beautiful gift.

☆ Give alternative gifts. For example, call up a friend you don't see often and set a firm date to spend time together instead of exchanging wrapped presents. Or have a recycled Christmas, where each family member chooses something he or she already owns to pass on to another. Or shop at thrift stores or garage sales. (Save this idea for sympathetic family members.)

The cost of mailing gifts can be a significant factor in your overall gift expenses. Here are some ways to trim this hidden expense:

☆ Make sure that you are mailing your packages by the most economical method. You may save plenty of dollars. We did a little research in our area during the Christmas season of 1981 and came up with a wide range of prices for sending a ten-pound package from coast to coast by bus, the United Parcel Service, and the U.S. Postal Service, as noted in the table below.

		UPS		*U.S. Postal Service*		
Carrier:	***Greyhound***	Common Carrier	Blue Label	Parcel Post	Priority Mail	Express Mail
Cost:	**$16.10**	**$4.79**	**$12.44**	**$6.62**	**$11.50**	**$20.50**
Days:	7–10	6–7	2	8–10	3–4	2

Note: for an additional $2.75, UPS will pick up the package. You only need to pay this extra charge once a week. If you mailed all your Christmas packages in the same week, your total pick-up charge would be $2.75.

The best way to get current information is to call your post office and other mail services and ask them to send you a copy of their rate charts.

☆ For packages weighing less than twenty-five pounds, it's generally cheaper to use the UPS, and in most cases they arrive sooner. If your package weighs more than twenty-five pounds, however, the Postal Service will usually deliver it for less. (Delivery time may be a day or two longer.)

☆ Mail early and avoid rush mailing charges. This is especially important for heavy packages, because the heavier your package, the greater the difference between Priority Mail and Parcel Post. For example, it would cost only $1.09 more to mail a two-pound package by Priority Mail, but it would cost $11.86 *more* to send a twenty-pound package by the faster route.

☆ Think "lightweight" when you are making up your gift list for faraway relatives. A one-pound package might cost $2.48 to mail by Parcel Post and a fifteen-pound package $8.48. Some suggestions: jewelry, photographs, prints, pens, pocketknives, posters, paperback books, tea, herbs, watches, lingerie, silk scarves, records, cassette tapes, calendars, magazine subscriptions, money, memberships, gift certificates.

You can also save money on gift-wrapping. Here are some ideas:

☆ Take along your pocket calculator when you buy your wrapping supplies. There may be a great difference in price among products of similar quality. You may save as much as one dollar per package. In general, it's best to buy 125-foot rolls of ribbon, large tubes of gift wrap, and strapping tape that meets Postal Service standards but does not exceed them (unless you are sending especially heavy packages).

☆ Tie your packages with colorful yarn. It's less expensive than ribbon and does not crumple in the mail. If you buy the yarn in the arts and crafts section rather than the gift wrap department, you can save even more money.

☆ If you are superorganized, buy your supplies for the future during post-Christmas sales. And if you're really cutting corners, iron last year's wrapping paper and ribbon and use again.

☆ Forget kraft (plain brown) outer wrap and mailing labels on your boxes and save yourself both time and money. The Postal Service and UPS prefer unwrapped packages sealed with strapping tape and with addresses written directly on the box.

SAVING TIME

When you add up all the time you spend thinking of gifts, shopping for them, making them, gift-wrapping them, boxing them for the mail, and hauling them to the post office, you probably have at least a week of concentrated effort. And if you make most of your gifts, you can triple that figure.

If you have the time to relax and enjoy all the details, gift-giving can be the best part of Christmas. But if you have to squeeze all those chores into an already full schedule, the pressure can cancel out the joy.

Here are some ways to spend less time on the mechanical aspects of giving:

☆ Give gift certificates, season tickets, movie tickets, magazine subscriptions (if you didn't send away for the subscriptions soon enough for a copy to arrive on Christmas, wrap up the current issue along with a note), or memberships. These gifts can often be taken care of with one phone call.

☆ Make your gift a tradition. Send the same thing each year and eliminate the time spent searching for the perfect gift. If people enjoy your gift and can count on it year after year, it becomes an important part of the holiday season. Some suggestions: a yearly renewal of a favorite magazine, a box of nuts or top-quality produce, season tickets to a favorite concert series.

☆ Give specialty food products delivered by mail.

☆ Eliminate time-consuming trips to the post office: have the UPS pick up your packages.

☆ If you mail your packages, plan your visits to the post office for the least busy hour, 10–11 A.M., and aim for Thursday, often the slowest day of the week.

☆ Do all your shopping through a book club or in one trip to a bookstore where you will find books to interest every person on your list. (Also, books can be easily slipped into mailers, eliminating the need for more elaborate packaging.)

☆ Stockpile your gifts and wrap them all at once. Set up an efficient wrapping center and wrap everything with the same paper and ribbon. Before you begin, be sure you have scissors, transparent tape, wrapping paper, tissue paper, gift cards (bought or homemade), boxes, and strapping tape. Get the whole family to help.

☆ Shop in stores that offer to wrap and mail your gifts.

☆ Buy colorful Christmas boxes, tie with ribbon, and skip the wrapping paper.

☆ Buy one big gift for an entire family rather than one for each individual and save time on the brainstorming, shopping, wrapping, and mailing.

☆ And the potentially biggest time and money saver of all: shop by catalog. In recent years you have probably noticed a big increase in the number of Christmas catalogs that find their way in to your mailbox. Now you can buy everything from diamonds to rubber boots without leaving home. In many cases you can call a toll-free number, place your order, read off your credit card number, and have the packages delivered to your door or, better yet, right to the recipient. You really *can* do all your Christmas shopping in a matter of hours, while taking advantage of direct-mail savings at the same time. You will also be able to make better choices because you can shop without pressure, and you will find it easier to keep track of the total bill and reconsider if you exceed your overall limit. (See the following section for a list of useful catalogs.)

GIFT CATALOGS

When you shop through catalogs, there are a few things to keep in mind. Many businesses will not process your order until your check clears, and that may take two weeks. To avoid delays, send money orders or pay with a credit card. Second, when you send along enclosures (checks or coins) be sure to indicate that in writing so they will not be overlooked. Third, date your letter and keep a photocopy or carbon in case there are any problems. Fourth, when your package arrives, examine the contents immediately to make sure the items have not been damaged and that you got what you ordered.

If you'd like a list of over six hundred catalogs, send away for *The Great Catalog Guide*, a free publication issued annually by the Direct Mail Marketing Association (DMMA). To get your copy of the guide, send seventy-five cents for postage to: *The Great Catalog Guide*, DMMA, Dept. WD, 6 East 43rd St., New York, NY 10017.

Some of our favorite mail-order catalogs are listed below to make your Christmas shopping easier. (For catalogs from UNICEF and other nonprofit organizations, see page 214.)

Eddie Bauer
This catalog is one of the classics. "Keeping people warm and comfortable has been our speciality since 1920." Here you will find a host of outdoor clothes, including hunting coats, vests, parkas of every description, goose-down face masks for next

year's Himalayan vacation, and a wide range of boots. There are also a few more cosmopolitan offerings, like lounging robes and Icelandic-wool car coats. To order, call toll free 800-426-6253 (in Alaska, Hawaii, Washington, and foreign countries, call 206-885-3330). Or write to: Eddie Bauer, 5th and Union, P.O. Box 3700, Seattle, WA 98124.

Garnet Hill: The Natural Fibers Catalog
Beautiful high-quality clothes, linen, and blankets made from natural fibers for those with discerning tastes and good incomes. Some items available: merino wool tights, flannel pj's, pure wool long underwear, silk stockings, and pure cotton garter belts. To order a catalog, call 603-823-5545 or write to: Garnet Hill, Franconia, NH 03580.

Home Food Systems
More than just a catalog, this is a manual that explains how to make cheese and milk sheep, how to choose ducks and geese for your farm. It will also tell you where to order quality grain mills, pasta makers, juicers, dehydrators, and canning equipment. It was published by Rodale Press of Emmaus, Pennsylvania, in 1981.

The International Cook's Catalogue
Inside this work by James Beard, Milton Glaser, and Burton Wolf you will find information on how to order cooking equipment you will never find in the aisles of your local supermarket, including Syrian copper frying pans, champagne pliers, Bain-Marie pans, and truffle cutters (in case you've lost your old ones), as well as a few mundane tools of the trade like coffee makers and sauerkraut crocks. *The International Cook's Catalogue* was published in 1977 by Random House, New York.

L. L. Bean
Snowshoes, gabardine slacks, touring caps, sleeping bags, tents, parkas, boots—*L. L. Bean* is another country-gentleman and

outdoorsman classic. To order a catalog, call 207-865-3161 between 8 A.M. and 4:30 P.M. eastern standard time, or write to: L. L. Bean, Customer Service, Freeport, ME 04033.

The Museum of Modern Art Bookstore and Gift Shop Catalog
The MOMA catalog has art books, prints, cards, exhibition-related material, and copies of many of the originals in MOMA's Design Collection. To order, call 212-956-7262 or write to: The Museum of Modern Art, 11 West 53rd St., New York, NY 10019.

Shop New York by Mail
"Buy from New York shops without hassling travel, crowds or subway." Catalogs from hundreds of famous New York retail stores are listed in this book. A Print Project Book from Avon Books, New York, published in 1981.

Tiffany and Company
For three dollars (prices may change) you can have your very own Tiffany's catalog, with over two hundred pages of jewelry, watches, crystal, and glass. For the select few. To order, call 212-755-8000 or write to: Tiffany and Company, 727 5th Ave., New York, NY 10022.

The Wholesale-by-Mail Catalog
"Over three hundred and fifty companies where you can buy almost anything at 30% to 90% off retail prices by MAIL!" In this bargain hunter's catalog by Lowell Miller you will find items as diverse as art and antiques, art materials, automotive and marine supplies, cosmetics, and medical equipment. St. Martin's Press in New York published it in 1979.

Williams-Sonoma: A Catalog for Cooks
This catalog features quality kitchen equipment and supplies at reasonable prices—much of it from France. Some typical

listings: heavy French aluminum roasting pans, cook's aprons from a restaurant supply house, two-and-a-half-pound wheels of Stilton cheese, quiche pans, and madeleine plaques. For the gourmet on your list. This catalog is free. Write to: Williams-Sonoma, Mail Order Dept., P.O. Box 3792, San Francisco, CA 94119.

ALTERNATIVE GIFT IDEAS

Many people are feeling a need to find alternatives to commercial gift-giving. The alternative gift ideas in this section cover a lot of ground. They include classic gift ideas that are often overlooked in the scramble for this year's hottest fads. There are also gifts of service, easy homemade gifts requiring little time or talent, unusual store-bought gifts, and gift ideas to spark your imagination. The gifts are grouped in age ranges.

☆ Gift ideas for children:

When you shop for children, look for toys that are durable, washable, have no sharp points or edges, encourage peaceful, creative play, and continue to be useful even when some of the pieces get lost.

Buy safe toys. Check for the mark "PS 72-76," indicating that the toy conforms to the voluntary safety standards established by the toy industry. If you have more questions about toy safety, call the U.S. Consumer Product Safety Commission on its toll-free hotline: 800-638-8326.

You will find that most toys are labeled according to age range, but toy experts say that most manufacturers "label up," which means they recommend that toys be used by slightly older children than is truly appropriate. For a more realistic estimate, take six months off the lower age number and a year off the top.

The suggestions that follow are for a mixture of simple, classic toys and more novel gift ideas.

☆ *Infants:*
Cloth blocks
Clutch ball
Crib gym
Mobile (The windup kind that plays music is more entertaining.)
Rubber teether
Baby mirror (made of unbreakable steel)
Plastic key ring
Stuffed animal
Bristle Blocks (Infants like to chew on them. Older ones can stick them together.)
Suction toy for the high chair

A gift for new parents: *A Sigh of Relief: The First-Aid Handbook for Childhood Emergencies,* by Martin Green (New York: Bantam Books, 1977). This book has been thoughtfully designed to be used by parents, babysitters, and others in an actual emergency. Large-print, easy-to-find-and-follow instructions help you deal with common childhood emergencies.

☆ *One- to three-year-olds:*
Tiny nesting boxes
Appliance box with doors and windows cut in it
Box of gummed labels
Box of adhesive bandages
Real flashlight and batteries
Collection of improvised bath toys (a plastic funnel, a turkey baster, an empty plastic shampoo bottle, plastic measuring spoons and cups, etc.)
Piggy bank with starter money
Homemade Play-Doh
Hinged objects
Pull toy

Riding toy
Stuffed animal
Wooden stringing beads
Blocks
Ball
Milk-bottle carrier
Stacking toy
Pounding toy
Shape sorter
Truck
Car
Doll
Plastic building blocks (large)
Wooden knob puzzle
Modeling clay

Gift-wrapping ideas for toddlers: tie bells to ribbon and make the paper easy to unwrap.

Make your toy gifts. Send away for a free booklet from the government called *Toys: Fun in the Making.* Write to: United States Government Printing Office, Dept. 76, Washington, DC 20401.

☆ *Four- to six-year-olds:*
Deck of cards
Homemade balance beam
Map of the town with the child's own house, school, mommy's and daddy's offices, church, library, zoo, etc., highlighted
Old suitcase filled with play clothes (veils, scarves, belts, hats, a nurse's hat, an apron, a tie, etc.)
Costume jewelry
Ticket for a ride on a real train
Banner with the child's name on it
Office supplies in a homemade executive kit

Art supplies
Strong magnet
Magnifying glass
Bird feeder
Magazine subscription (see the following suggestions)
Sewing kit
Harmonica, drum set, or slide flute
Real brass bell
Simple book about the child that you wrote and illustrated
Real stethoscope (available at medical supply houses)
Puzzle (up to a hundred pieces)
Play people
Dolls and dollhouse
Building blocks (small)
Paint and easel
Simple board or card game
Picture book
Record
Cassette tape
Tricycle or bike
Slinky

☆ *Grade-school children:*
Magazine subscription. Here are four children's magazines that received high marks from librarians and teachers:

Cricket has been called "the only truly literary publication for children ages 6–12." Its editorial board includes Isaac Bashevis Singer, Paul Heins, and Lloyd Anderson. *Cricket* features articles, stories, and illustrations by internationally known writers and illustrators. It's fifteen dollars. Write to: *Cricket,* Box 2670, Boulder, CO 80302.

Ranger Rick's Nature Magazine features activities and information to help children aged five to twelve enjoy nature and appreciate the need for conservation. To subscribe, you need to pay $10.50 in membership dues to the National Wildlife Federation plus an additional $7.00 subscription fee. Write to: *Ranger Rick,* National Wildlife Federation, 1412 16th St., N.W., Washington, DC 20036.

Stone Soup is a collection of stories, poems, book reviews, and drawings done by children aged six to twelve for children of the same age. A subscription costs seven dollars. Write to: *Stone Soup,* Children's Art Foundation, P.O. Box 83, Santa Cruz, CA 95063.

World is a children's magazine with the same beautiful photography as its parent magazine, *National Geographic,* and treats many of the same subjects. Recommended for children aged eight to twelve. It's a bargain at $6.95. Write to: *World,* National Geographic Society, Dept. 00581, 17th and M Sts., N.W., Washington, DC 20013.

More gift ideas for grade-school children:

Ticket to a favorite sporting event
Real sports equipment
Book of movie tickets
Homemade sewing kit
Embroidery hoop, material, needles, and embroidery thread
Leaf press
Scrapbook
Music lessons
Simple instrument
Calendar
Science kit
Knitting needles and yarn
Crochet hook and yarn
Real cooking equipment
Video or computer game

Science project
Aquarium
Weather equipment
Hand-held calculator
Shares of stock
One-egg chick incubator (available in science stores)
Simple camera and photo album
Pocket Tinker Toys
Three-dimensional puzzle
Coin or stamp collecting album

In the December 1981 issue of *Consumer Reports,* the editors published a survey of the favorite board games of 1,278 eight- to twelve-year-olds. Here are the top ten in order: Monopoly, Life, the Mad Magazine Game, Clue, Othello, Stratego, chess, Touché, backgammon, and Master Mind.

☆ *Teen-agers:*

Donation to a favorite charity (Save the Whales, etc.)
UNICEF concert records
Music lessons
Book of movie tickets
Telephone credit
Session with a cosmetic expert
Credit at a bookstore
Credit at a record store
Photography lessons
Sports lessons
Cooking lessons
Blank book for a journal
Book on drawing, pencils, and art paper
Special lunch or dinner at a nice restaurant
Calligraphy pen and an instruction book
Record (Get suggestions about a favorite recording star.)
Cassette tape for the car

Dictionary
Furniture for the teen-ager's room
Sheets or a down comforter
Sports equipment
Camping equipment
Subscription to a magazine in a prospective career field, or one of general interest
Invitation to a ballet, play, or concert
Ten dollars in quarters for video games
Shares of stock
Money

☆ *Adults:*

If you would like to give out-of-the-ordinary gifts, shop at out-of-the-ordinary stores and sources, like:

Marine supply stores
Government surplus stores
Import stores
Restaurant supply stores
Antique stores
Museum shops
Arts and crafts galleries
Damaged-freight stores
Stationery stores
Classified ads
Garage sales
Plant nurseries
Hardware stores
Health food stores

Further a fantasy—give a subscription to a magazine or a book on a secret ambition (for example: *Writer's Digest* for a budding writer, or a book on inventions for a would-be inventor)

Telephone credit
Collection of favorite family recipes
Collection of small things that the person habitually loses (pens, safety pins, scissors, Scotch tape, etc.)
Address and phone number of a lost friend or relative
One-hour body rub
Offer to babysit for a weekend in the person's house
Complete emergency dinner for the freezer
Saturday work party for an older relative
Cater to a secret indulgence—a subscription to a movie magazine for someone who only buys them on the sly, a big hunk of quality French baking chocolate
Collection of traditional holiday recipes for a grown-up son or daughter
Aerial map of the area (available from: National Cartographic Information Center, 507 National Center, Reston, VA 22092—phone 703-860-6045 for more information)
Your family genealogy
Enlarged pictures from old negatives
Catalog from a local community college plus money for the course of the person's choice
Classical Christmas record (see suggestions under Music)
Copy of this book
Weather equipment
Calligraphy pens plus an instruction book
Professional chef's equipment
Specialty food from your part of the country
Family magazine subscription
Load of firewood
Armload of greens

A special gift for northwesterners: an airplane tour of Mount St. Helens. For $29.95 per person you can spend an hour in a charter plane flying over the crater, Spirit Lake, and the Toutle River

Valley. For more information call AAR Western Skyways at 503-665-1181.

A gift for all your friends with young children: a Christmas party for their children the Saturday before Christmas. They can drop the kids off and have three or four precious hours to shop, wrap, bake, and decorate. You may want to help the children make Christmas cards for their parents; wrapping paper with shelf paper, tempera paint, and potato-block prints; or salt-dough ornaments (see Food for directions).

☆ Gift Ideas for Men (We single out men because so many people find them harder to shop for.)

Photography or darkroom equipment
Season pass to a favorite sport
Traditional holiday food from his childhood
For a sailor: marine maps
For a hunter: topographical maps
Binoculars
Bird or plant identification book
Bottle of port from his birth year (could be very expensive) or other wine
Subscription to a science magazine
One free music lesson on the instrument of his choice
One free flying lesson
Ski lift tickets
Professional chef's equipment
Cookbook
Gift certificate for L. L. Bean or Eddie Bauer
Backpacking equipment
Deluxe first-aid kit for boat, camper, car, or backpacking trips
Gardening book
Outdoor plant
One night (with you) in a hotel

Pasta machine
Sausage stuffer and sausage cookbook
Japanese saws and knives
Pruning equipment
His horoscope
Telescope
Star chart
Book about space
Rowboat
Plastic raft
Rubber raft
Ticket for a white-water rafting trip
Print for his office
Gift certificate for a stereo store
Coupon good for an absolutely free weekend somewhere
Enlarged photo of the house where he spent his childhood
Microscope
Horseback-riding lessons
Tennis lessons
Case of tennis balls
Home computer ($)
Pool table ($)

☆ Gifts for Older Folks:
Take them Christmas shopping
Run errands for them
Have a housecleaning or repair party
Invite them to your house for singing or cookie-baking
Set a monthly library or shopping and lunch date
For people with poor eyesight:
- Playing cards with jumbo numbers
- Large-type books
- The large-type edition of *The New York Times*
- Volunteer to read to them

☆ Family Gifts

If you pick gifts the whole family can enjoy, you will not only simplify your shopping, but help bring that family closer together.

Inexpensive gifts:

Two decks of cards and a book of card-game rules
Classic board game—nose around to see which ones they have first
Five-hundred-piece jigsaw puzzle
Three-dimensional puzzle
Badminton set
Magazine subscription
Inner tubes
Sled
Soccer ball
Basketball hoop
Dictionary
Globe
Dwarf fruit tree

More expensive family gifts:

Cider press
Food dehydrator
Ice cream maker
Pasta machine
Telescope
Binoculars
Microscope
Archery equipment
Grain mill
Tent
Potter's wheel
Rubber raft
Ski lift tickets

☆ Easy Homemade Gifts:

Many people want to give homemade gifts but don't feel they have the time and/or talent to do the conventional holiday crafts. Here are some gifts that require few special skills and can be as simple or elaborate as you choose to make them:

1. Special Family Blend Tea and Coffee
Buy several of your favorite teas or types of coffee beans in bulk. Come home and experiment with different blends. Call the family in for a taste test and have everyone vote for his or her favorite. The winner is your "Family Blend." Make up a big batch, scoop it into bags, and tie them with ribbons. (Do you have extra time? Design family labels.)

2. Cracked Nuts
If you live in a part of the country where nuts are plentiful, give your friends sacks of cracked nuts. Buy them in bulk in a produce store, or look for a you-pick-it farm in the classified section of your newspaper. Bring the nuts home and crack them in front of the fire. Have little children search for shells in the pile of shelled nuts. Scoop them into sacks and tie with ribbons, or deliver in a woven basket. (These make wonderful early Christmas gifts.)

3. Roasted Nuts
Buy or gather almonds, hazelnuts, cashews, and/or filberts. Shell. Spread on a cookie sheet, sprinkle with salt, and bake in a 350-degree oven for five to twenty minutes depending on size. Deliver in small baskets, pottery, or plastic sacks with ribbon.

4. Family Cookbook (requires advance planning)
Send a photocopied letter to all your family members asking them for a favorite recipe in their own careful handwriting. Ask them to write on the same sheet of paper a little about the recipe (for example, its history or an amusing anecdote). When you have a collection of recipes, photocopy the original letters. (If you are pressed for time, look for a copier that collates and staples.) The layout can be as simple or as elaborate as you care to make it. This gift will be appreciated by friends as well as family.

5. Family Calendar
Write, duplicate, and send out a letter to all your relatives asking them for their birth dates, their anniversaries, and the dates of any historic family events (for example, the birth dates of important ancestors, dates when they immigrated or made important moves, and so on). When you have the responses, buy a blank calendar at a stationer's and enter all the events. Take the completed calendar to a printer and have it reproduced. (For a more elaborate production, add historic or current family photographs to the calendar, but plan on paying for a more expensive printing process.)

6. Family Tree
Make an up-to-the-minute family tree complete with birth dates, current addresses, and phone numbers. If you have no drawing skills, simply supply the data in chart form. But if you are artistic, enter the information on a big family tree.

7. The Gift of Spring
Give the gift of springtime: a pot of blooming narcissus. (You have to start about two months ahead of time for this one.) Directions for forcing: fill a shallow container with rocks or decorative pebbles and add water until it reaches just below the surface. Set bulbs on the gravel and add more pebbles to hold them upright. Set the container next to a window, away from direct heat. As the leaves appear, rotate the container so the bulbs will grow evenly. The flowers will bloom in four to six weeks and will last two weeks at room temperature. (The bulbs cannot be repotted.)

ALTERNATIVE GIFT SOURCES

The following nonprofit organizations make part of their income by selling Christmas gifts to the public. When you buy gifts from these agencies, the profit goes to benefit their causes. We describe them in sufficient detail so that you can decide which ones you wish to support with your Christmas dollars.

International Program for Human Resource Development (IPHRD)

IPHRD helps self-help groups in more than forty countries market their handicrafts and other products in the United States. With the income generated through sales they support a dairy development project, an agricultural development project, and small industrial projects, all within the context of an integrated rural development program. "We are a development organization, managed and developed by people of the Third World."

IPHRD will send you free mail-order catalogs. Request any of the following catalogs: wood carvings, jewelry, boxes, papier-mâché, onyx, traditional musical instruments, brass. Send your request to: IPHRD/Mail Order, P.O. Box 30216, Bethesda, MD 20014.

Koinonia Farm

This group is committed to living out the radical teachings of Jesus—peace, human kindness, sharing, and simplicity. Part of its support comes from the sale of quality pecan and peanut products. For example, you may order Box A—a two-and-a-quarter-pound round fruitcake in a tin, a twelve-ounce box of pecan-stuffed dates, a seven-ounce box of milk chocolate pecan candy, and a one-pound box of select pecan halves—by sending $14.45 to Koinonia Farm, Route 2, Americus, GA 31709. The group will also be glad to send you more information on its life and work.

Match

Match is a regional Appalachian marketing coalition made up of thirty low-income craft groups from eight Appalachian states, which provides technical, administrative, and marketing aid to over eight thousand craftsmen. Its goals are to develop group self-sufficiency and independence by cooperative action, to alleviate hunger, and to bring about change through human and community development. For a catalog with full details of craft items and for more information about Match, send a self-addressed, stamped envelope to: Match, Inc., P.O. Box 68, Berea, KY 40403.

The Other Side/Jubilee
This organization imports and sells indigenous handicrafts produced by worker-owned Christian cooperatives in Bangladesh, Colombia, the Dominican Republic, and Haiti. Send for the free retail catalog: The Other Side/Jubilee, Inc., Box 12236, Philadelphia, PA 19144.

Sales Exchange for Refugee Rehabilitation Vocations (SERRV)
SERRV is an ecumenical church-related marketing program, created to serve overseas artisans who can produce high-quality, salable handicrafts and need to sell them as a means of livelihood, but who otherwise would not have adequate sales outlets for their products. SERRV handicrafts come from approximately fifty developing countries around the world. The price paid to the producer-supplier consists of about half of the retail selling price. The other half goes for essential overhead, including customs duty, transportation, handling costs, salaries for the administrative staff, shipping, and sales functions. In 1980 SERRV sales totaled $1,821,834. Approximately 74 percent of these sales were made through churches, service groups, and stores that resell SERRV handicrafts. The craft items available for sale change from year to year, but the basic products fall into these categories: handcrafted jewelry, ethnic clothing, home furnishings, and holiday accessories.

SERRV does not offer a retail, mail-order catalog. To find the retail outlet nearest you, call the national headquarters (301-635-2255) or send a stamped, self-addressed envelope to: SERRV, P.O. Box 365, New Windsor, MD 21776. If your church or organization is interested in becoming a distributor of SERRV handicrafts, write to SERRV and ask for the resale packet.

The Self-Help Program

This program is sponsored by the Mennonite Central Committee. Like SERRV, it solicits handicrafts from developing countries and pays the individual producers a fair price for items such as baskets and plant hangers from Bangladesh, hand-carved wood from Haiti and the Philippines, and embroidered linen made by Palestinian refugees. "We are a relief and service agency seeking to meet human need in the name of Christ."

The program markets its crafts through state fairs, church bazaars, and nonprofit organizations. To find the nearest retailer, call 717-738-1101, or send a stamped, self-addressed envelope to: Self-Help Program, Mennonite Central Committee, 21 South 12th St., Akron, PA 17501.

United Nations International Children's Emergency Fund (UNICEF)

UNICEF concerns itself with the essential needs and problems of children, primarily those in developing countries. It helps plan and assists child-care programs that are the responsibility of individual countries themselves. It is the policy of UNICEF to help children of both sides in an international conflict.

You undoubtedly are familiar with UNICEF Christmas cards. Each year UNICEF sells over a hundred million cards in more than a hundred countries, providing it with annual revenue of about fifteen million dollars. But you may not be aware that UNICEF also markets toys, books, games, calendars, and year-round greeting cards. These gifts are designed to acquaint people with cultures around the world, and the profits go to help children all over the earth. To find the location of the UNICEF outlet closest to you, look up UNICEF in your phone book or call toll free 800-228-1666 (in Nebraska, 800-642-8787). Or write for a card and gift catalog: *The Winter Collection,* U.S. Committee for UNICEF, 331 East 38th St., New York, NY 10016.

* * *

In addition to these listings, the *Alternative Celebrations Catalogue* has a state-by-state, eight-page section listing self-help craft projects. To order this valuable resource, send five dollars to: Alternatives, 1924 East 3rd St., Bloomington, IN 47401.

ALTERNATIVE CHRISTMAS ACTIVITIES FOR CHURCHES

Over the years, we have kept a list of ideas that churches around the country have come up with to make their church programming more consistent with the spiritual meaning of Christmas. Scan the following list for ideas that your church might adapt, or use the list to stimulate your own brainstorming.

IDEAS TO REACH OUT TO OTHER PEOPLE

- ☆ Have a "Living, Giving Tree." Encourage families within the church to give a gift for the needy. Place the wrapped present under a living Christmas tree in a prominent place in the church.
- ☆ Begin the Christmas season with an undecorated Christmas tree. Each family that does an act that expresses the Christmas spirit is entitled to bring an ornament to put on the tree. At the end of the season the brightly decorated tree will be a testament to the commnity's goodwill toward others.
- ☆ Have someone make a large poster of the Christmas Pledge (see page 17) and tack it in a central location in the church. Leave room for church members to sign.
- ☆ As a church community, adopt a needy family.
- ☆ Have each willing member of the congregation choose a "secret friend," some friend or acquaintance to help out in

some manner at some time during the holiday season. For example, help clean the house of an older person in anticipation of holiday visits.

☆ Put special ornaments on the church Christmas tree with the names of the people in the congregation who are sick, housebound, or in a nursing home, and could use a friendly visit or help with holiday chores.

IDEAS TO UNITE THE CHURCH COMMUNITY

☆ Have a single-parent greens-gathering party.

☆ Have children interview their grandparents for stories of Christmas long ago. Print the stories in a special church newsletter.

☆ Have a "Fathers-and-Children Wrapping Session." Ask all the fathers and their children to bring family presents and wrapping paper to a special gathering. This will not only help out their wives but bring the men and their children closer together.

☆ Start a special campaign to visit church members who are in nursing homes and hospitals.

☆ Choose people to help with Christmas programming who can use more social interaction, rather than those who are already overcommitted.

IDEAS TO REDUCE COMMERCIALISM

☆ Exchange gifts on St. Nicholas's Day (December 6) rather than Christmas Eve or Christmas Day, to save the true holiday for religious expression.

☆ Pledge not to exchange Christmas gifts with people within the congregation. Donate this money to a worthwhile cause.

☆ Have a church Christmas card for everyone to sign. As a symbolic statement that the earth's resources should be preserved, do not exchange cards with people within the congregation.
☆ Cut Christmas expenditures by 10 percent.
☆ Have a "Santa's Workshop." Each family donates a small gift or homemade present to a special children's bazaar. Each child brings a small amount of money and buys presents for other people in the family. (Gifts may be fifty cents apiece, for example.) The money goes to the church or some other worthwhile cause. This gives children the privilege of giving and keeps their presents to family members a secret.
☆ Pledge to reduce your children's television viewing during the holiday season and replace those hours with family activities. Organize a discussion of commercialism versus the spirit of Christmas in the Sunday school.
☆ As a congregation, pledge to shop at those stores that delay their Christmas decorating until after Thanksgiving.
☆ Have an alternative Christmas tree that members can decorate with written ideas for a simpler Christmas.
☆ Make a banner that says TAKE TIME OF KEEP IT SIMPLE and hang it in the church foyer.
☆ Each week of Advent, church bulletins could offer practical suggestions for carrying out each of the five ideas of the Christmas Pledge.

IDEAS FOR CHURCH PROGRAMMING

☆ Sponsor an "Unplug the Christmas Machine" group workshop, the four-hour workshop on which this book has been based. Through this workshop, your church will help its members determine the changes they need to make to have a more rewarding, spiritual celebration. The eighty-five-page *Leader's Guide* contains everything your church or organization needs to successfully and easily conduct the workshop. No additional training for the leader is needed. To obtain your copy of the *Leader's Guide*, send a check for thirty-five dollars made out to Robinson/Staeheli to Family Celebrations, P.O. Box 06517, Portland, OR 97206. (Also, you may write to this address with specific questions about the workshop.)

☆ Offer a Christmas planning workshop to the congregation in early fall. The purpose of the workshop is to explore the church's role in the celebration. The session could follow this format:

1. List the church's traditional Christmas activities and consider these questions: Who is responsible for planning and carrying each one out? Who is each of the programs designed to benefit? Which work well?
2. What should the church's goals be at Christmas? Take some time to dream about creative ways the church could be a more positive force in restoring the meaning of the celebration. How well do your current holiday activities further your goals?
3. Formulate specific ways to reach these goals. You may wish to take these questions into consideration: How can the work involved in these activities be redistributed to relieve hard-working church members and include new, lonely, or single people? How can ongoing church responsibilities be reduced so that church leaders can spend more time with their families? How can church sermons and education classes reinforce the ideas generated in this planning session?

MAKING A CHRISTMAS BUDGET

In an ideal world, people wouldn't have to think about money at Christmas. Adults could go through the holiday season as carefree as children and with no awareness of how the celebration translated into dollars and cents. Unfortunately, many adults not only have to think about money at Christmas, but worry about it as well. They worry about whether they have enough money to travel to see their relatives. They wonder if they can afford to buy their children the gifts they really want. And they find that they have to cut back on many of their holiday plans so that there will be enough money left over for everyday expenses.

But despite this worrying and economizing, many families still end up spending more money at Christmas than they can comfortably afford. We have found that setting up a holiday budget is a good way to keep your Christmas expenses under control. The first step in this process is to get a realistic picture of how you have been spending money in the past. Most people greatly underestimate how much money they spend at Christmas because there are scores of common but hidden holiday expenses. People not only spend money for obvious things like gifts, holiday food, and decorations, but also pay for a lot of "incidentals." On the following pages you will find a list of typical holiday purchases. Take a few moments to place a check mark by each of the items you spent money on last year. No one family would have all of these expenses, but most people have more of them than they realize.

Gifts

☆ Store-bought gifts
☆ Craft supplies to make gifts
☆ Wrapping paper
☆ Tissue paper
☆ Ribbon
☆ Bows
☆ Professional gift-wrapping
☆ Gift tags
☆ Brown paper for mailing
☆ Gift boxes

☆ Strapping tape
☆ Transparent tape
☆ Mailing costs
☆ Transportation for shopping
☆ Catalogs
☆ Other

Food

☆ Special kitchen equipment (plum pudding molds, Christmas cookie cutters, etc.)
☆ Baking ingredients (candied fruits, dates, nuts, butter, liquor, etc.)
☆ More convenience foods and restaurant meals because of busier schedules
☆ Extra food for holiday guests and parties
☆ Christmas Eve food ingredients
☆ Christmas dinner ingredients
☆ New Year's dinner ingredients
☆ Liquor
☆ Special holiday food for your family (eggnog, fresh fruit baskets, nuts, etc.)

Entertaining

☆ Professional housecleaning
☆ Professional rug-cleaning
☆ Professional yard work
☆ Catering
☆ Home repairs and remodeling
☆ Invitations
☆ Extra cleaning products
☆ Extra glasses, plates, silver, serving dishes, table linen
☆ Flowers
☆ Candles
☆ Other special decorations
☆ Party clothes

☆ Dry cleaning
☆ New furniture
☆ New houseplants

Houseguests

☆ New linen (towels, sheets, pillowcases)
☆ Pillows, blankets
☆ Higher utility bills
☆ Home repairs
☆ Entertainment (movies, dinners out, museums, concerts)
☆ Extra transportation costs
☆ Toys and games for visiting children

Travel

☆ Cost of transportation (airfare, train tickets, gasoline, etc.)
☆ Car rental once you reach your destination
☆ Lodging
☆ Meals out
☆ Souvenirs
☆ Guidebooks
☆ Maps
☆ House gifts
☆ Games and toys for children while traveling
☆ Books and magazines for adults
☆ Disposable diapers
☆ Pet boarding
☆ Timed lights and burglar alarms for your house
☆ Travel insurance
☆ Luggage
☆ Car maintenance, supplies (chains, etc.), and repairs

Decorations

☆ Christmas tree
☆ Tree stand

☆ Lights
☆ Replacement bulbs
☆ Tree ornaments
☆ Outdoor wreath or wreath supplies
☆ Crèche
☆ Advent wreath
☆ Candles
☆ Other inside decorations
☆ Craft books and magazines
☆ Craft supplies
☆ Greens, cones, etc.
☆ Outdoor decorations

Christmas Cards

☆ The cards themselves
☆ Postage
☆ Photographs
☆ Copying or printing costs

Charity

☆ Increased church donations
☆ Donations to charity
☆ Other

Miscellaneous

☆ Long-distance phone calls
☆ Increased entertainment costs
☆ Film and camera supplies
☆ Camera
☆ Film developing
☆ New clothes and shoes
☆ Dry cleaning
☆ Haircuts
☆ Baby-sitting

☆ Wood for the fire
☆ Holiday tipping
☆ Christmas records, sheet music, or tapes
☆ Other

The next step in creating a holiday budget is to set a spending ceiling. (If you are married, involve your spouse in this decision.) Be realistic. Think about how much you spent last year and make any adjustments you feel are desirable.

Spending ceiling: $

Next, make some rough estimates of how you would like this money allocated and enter those figures in the following categories (don't worry about being too precise; these are only general indicators):

Food: $
Gifts: $
Entertaining guests: $
Travel: $
Charity: $
Family entertainment: $
Decorations: $
Miscellaneous: $

Finally, throughout the season, use the expense log that follows to keep a running tally of all your extra holiday expenses. From time to time, total up the various categories and compare your estimates with the actual figures. Then change your spending pattern if you see the need.

Actual Expense Log

Date	Item	Category	Cost	Running Total

Bibliography

I. The History and Sociology of Christmas

Barnett, James H. *The American Christmas: A Study in National Culture.* New York: Arno Press, 1976. A sociological study of the contemporary Christmas celebration and some of its connections with American society and culture.

Baur, John. *Christmas on the American Frontier.* Caldwell, Ida.: Caxton Printers, 1961. Firsthand accounts of the way Christmas was celebrated one hundred years ago.

Heller, Steven. *Artists' Christmas Cards.* New York: A & W Publishers, 1979. Christmas through the artist's eye.

Link, Mark. *The Merriest Christmas Book.* Niles, Ill.: Argus Communications, 1974. The author juxtaposes photos, poems, and quotations to guide the reader through an exploration of the history of Christmas.

Miall, Anthony and Peter. *The Victorian Christmas Book.* New York: Pantheon Books, 1978. A delightful description of Christmas in nineteenth-century Victorian England, incorporating photos, artwork, and newspaper and magazine accounts from the period.

Stevens, Patricia B. *Merry Christmas! A History of the Holiday.* New York: Macmillan Publishing Co., 1979. A history that begins with the Nativity and traces the development of familiar customs, through illustrations, songs, and anecdotes.

II. Family Christmas Crafts and Activities

Coskey, Evelyn. *Christmas Crafts for Everyone.* Nashville, Tenn.: Abingdon Press, 1976. A book of international craft-oriented Christmas activities, with clear instructions and illustrations. Helps teach children the customs of other countries.

Have a Natural Christmas. Emmaus, Pa.: Rodale Press, 1976. Simple things to make and bake for Christmas.

Miller, Margaret E., et al. *The Gift of Time: Family Activities for Advent, Christmas, Epiphany.* Wilton, Conn.: Morehouse-Barlow Co., 1977. A resource book for Christian families who want to take part in activities that bring into focus the true meaning of the holiday season.

Walker, Georgiana, ed. *The Celebration Book.* Glendale, Calif.: Regal Books, 1977. Ideas on how Christian families can celebrate the holidays.

III. How to Change Your Celebration

Alternate Celebrations Catalog. New York: Pilgrim Press, 1982. The people at Alternatives, a nonprofit corporation, have been crusading for a simpler Christmas for years. This two-hundred-page book explores alternative ways to celebrate, with the emphasis on simple living.

Pax, Noel. *Simply Christmas: How to Have a Non-Commercial Christmas.* New York: Walker & Co., 1980. Suggestions for eliminating the materialism of the celebration and concentrating on the religious meaning of Christmas, family life, and the expression of love.

Index

About the Authors

Jo Robinson and Jean Staeheli are free-lance writers who live in Portland, Oregon, with their husbands and young children. Their Christmas research began in 1978 when they were asked by an Oregon college to design a workshop to help families create more value-centered, rewarding celebrations. The *Leader's Guide* to their "Unplug the Christmas Machine" workshop has been purchased by community colleges, schools, social service agencies, and churches around the country. In addition to designing their workshop, they have written articles for *Redbook* magazine on how Christmas affects family life and have appeared on television and radio programs across the country, including the Phil Donahue show.